TABLE OF CONTENTS

Top 20 Test Taking Tips... 4
Theoretical Perspectives.. 5
Research Strategies and Methodology.. 9
Biological Development Throughout the Life Span...15
Perceptual Development Throughout the Life Span...30
Cognitive Development Throughout the Lifespan...34
Language Development...41
Intelligence Throughout the Life Span...49
Social Development Throughout the Life Span..52
Family, Home, and Society Throughout the Life Span..65
Personality and Emotion 73
Learning...76
Schooling, Work, and Interventions..78
Atypical Development...86
Practice Test...99
    Practice Questions..99
    Answer Key and Explanations...106
Secret Key #1 - Time is Your Greatest Enemy 112
    Pace Yourself 112
Secret Key #2 - Guessing is not Guesswork 113
    Monkeys Take the Test...113
    $5 Challenge...114
Secret Key #3 - Practice Smarter, Not Harder 115
    Success Strategy...115
Secret Key #4 - Prepare, Don't Procrastinate..116
Secret Key #5 - Test Yourself..117
General Strategies..118
Special Report: How to Overcome Test Anxiety 123
    Lack of Preparation...123
    Physical Signals 124
    Nervousness...124
    Study Steps...126
    Helpful Techniques 127
Special Report: Additional Bonus Material 132

Top 20 Test Taking Tips

1. Carefully follow all the test registration procedures
2. Know the test directions, duration, topics, question types, how many questions
3. Setup a flexible study schedule at least 3-4 weeks before test day
4. Study during the time of day you are most alert, relaxed, and stress free
5. Maximize your learning style; visual learner use visual study aids, auditory learner use auditory study aids
6. Focus on your weakest knowledge base
7. Find a study partner to review with and help clarify questions
8. Practice, practice, practice
9. Get a good night's sleep; don't try to cram the night before the test
10. Eat a well balanced meal
11. Know the exact physical location of the testing site; drive the route to the site prior to test day
12. Bring a set of ear plugs; the testing center could be noisy
13. Wear comfortable, loose fitting, layered clothing to the testing center; prepare for it to be either cold or hot during the test
14. Bring at least 2 current forms of ID to the testing center
15. Arrive to the test early; be prepared to wait and be patient
16. Eliminate the obviously wrong answer choices, then guess the first remaining choice
17. Pace yourself; don't rush, but keep working and move on if you get stuck
18. Maintain a positive attitude even if the test is going poorly
19. Keep your first answer unless you are positive it is wrong
20. Check your work, don't make a careless mistake

Theoretical Perspectives

Domains of development

Developmental psychologists outline three fundamental domain of development: cognitive, physical, and emotional-social. Cognitive developments are changes in thinking and reasoning, including the development of abstract thought, linguistic ability, and memory. Physical development is the set of changes in the human body, including both maturation and degeneration. The brain's development as an organ is included in physical development. Emotional-social development, finally, is the set of personality changes that affect a person's emotional development and social skills.

Main determinants of development

Personal development occurs through biological, cognitive, and socio-emotional processes. Biological processes are most apparent to the eye. These include changes in appearance, as well as changes in the physical structure of the brain and internal organs. Cognitive processes, on the other hand, have to do with the growth and decline of the reasoning faculty, as well as the use of language and numbers. Finally, socioemotional processes relate to interpersonal communication and the regulation of the emotions. These processes have to do with changes in the way a person relates to others and the way in which a person can govern his own feelings.

Piaget's cognitive developmental theory

4 stages intellectual development

The cognitive psychologist Piaget outlined four specific stages of intellectual development. In the sensorimotor stage, which lasts from birth to two years of age, the child begins to understand the link between sensation and motor behavior. Between the ages of two and seven, in what is known as the preoperational stage, the child begins to incorporate symbols, most importantly those used in language. Between the ages of seven and eleven, in what is known as the stage of concrete operations, the child develops primitive reason and learns concepts about size and number. In the stage of formal operations, which begins at age eleven and goes until adulthood, the child develops abstract reasoning and a systematic approach to learning.

(1) Sensorimotor birth-2
(2) preoperational 2-7
(3) concrete operations 7-11
(4) formal operations 11-adult

Nature vs. nurture

One of the fundamental debates in psychology is the extent to which human development is affected by heredity or environment. In the shorthand of psychology, this is known as the debate between nature and nurture. Advocates of the nature side believes that human development is regular and consistent, and motivated primarily by forces of biological change inside the human body. Those who take the nurture side, on the other hand, assert that the social and physical environments are the most important determinants of development. These professionals tend to focus on the influence of family, health, and community.

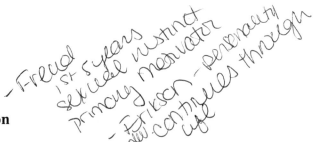
- Freud 1st 5 years sexual instinct primary motivator
- Erikson - personality dev continues through life

Basic ideas of Freud and Erikson

According to Freud, the first experiences in a person's life have a formative effect on his personality as an adult. In particular, the adult personality is formed by the resolution of the conflict between the desire for pleasure and the reality of insufficiency. For Freud, the sexual instinct is the primary motivator. Erikson, on the other hand, revised Freud's theory by expanding the sexual instinct into a more general desire for social interaction. Also contra Freud, Erikson suggested that personality development continues throughout life, rather than being restricted to the first five years.

Freudian stages of development

Freud 5 stages development

Sigmund Freud outlined five stages of psychosexual development: oral, anal, phallic, latency, and genital. During the oral stage, which lasts from birth to about 1.5 years of age, the child's primary focus of pleasure is his mouth. The anal stage lasts until the child is three years old, and is the stage in which the anus is the focus of pleasure. In the phallic stage, which runs from about the third to the sixth year, the child is preoccupied with his genitals. In the latency stage, which span from age six to puberty, sexual interest is put aside as the child's focus is on intellectual and social development. In puberty, however, which Freud called the genital stage, sexual interest reemerges and becomes focused on other people.

Erikson's stages of development

Erikson 8 stages (crises)

According to Erik Erikson, social context is key when considering personality development. Erikson delineated eight psychosocial stages and asserted that each of these stages is accompanied by a particular developmental challenge. In Erikson's terms, these "crises" give an individual the potential for major growth. Erikson also contended that there are points in a person's life when he or she must either develop parts of the personality or lose them. If these elements of the personality are lost, a malformation of the rest of the personality will result. Erikson's model was the first to address the entire span of life rather than just childhood and adolescence.

Erikson's stages of development are as follows:
- *1* Year one: trust versus mistrust - During this stage, the child determines whether his environment is a positive or negative place.
- *1-3* Years one to three: autonomy versus shame - A child begins to act independently, but may become doubtful if he is punished too much.
- *4+5* Years four and five: initiative versus guilt - The child begins to seek out information and become responsible for his behavior.
- *(6-puberty)* Year six to puberty: industry versus inferiority - The child begins to develop cognitive sophistication, though he may become discouraged.
- *adolescence* Adolescence: identity versus identity confusion - The child seeks to define his own identity.
- *early adulthood* Early adulthood: intimacy versus isolation - The person begins to establish close relationships.
- *middle adulthood* Middle adulthood: generativity versus stagnation - The person either continues to move forward and become more socially integrated or is inert.

late adulthood • Late adulthood: integrity versus despair - A person either solidifies a more complex personality or becomes overwhelmed by existential angst.

Maslow's hierarchy of needs

Psychologist Abraham Maslow listed human needs in terms of their relative importance. He depicted needs on a pyramid. The most important needs, at the base of the pyramid, must be satisfied before higher needs can be addressed. The needs at the bottom of the pyramid are things like shelter, food, water, and the desire for reproduction. After these needs are satisfied, a person can begin to address the needs for friendship, accomplishment, self-esteem, and community. At the very top of the pyramid is the need for self-actualization, which is the need to fully achieve personal potential.

Mechanistic and organismic models of development

Psychologists tend to either use the mechanistic or organismic model when discussing human development. According to the mechanistic model, human beings are merely physical objects in a well-ordered, logical universe. The mechanistic model of human development suggests that people change in gradual but continuous ways, in large part because of external influences. The organismic model, on the other hand, assigns much more agency to humans; it suggests that individuals are largely responsible for the changes in their own lives. The organismic model of human development declares that personal change occurs in discrete steps, and is not entirely motivated by external forces.

Continuity and discontinuity models of development

continuity model → learning
discontinuity model → defined stages
ex. Piaget
Freud
Erikson

According to the continuity model of human development, human beings change in steady, ongoing ways. Psychologists who subscribe to the continuity model of development believe that learning is a major determinant of behavior, and that learning occurs slowly over time. The discontinuity model, on the other hand, describes personality development as a series of defined stages, in which the ego and personae undergo measurable change. Famous versions of the discontinuity model include the developmental theories advanced by Piaget, Freud, and Erikson.

Vygotsky's sociocultural cognitive theory

Vygotsky - language

The Russian developmental psychologist Lev Vygotsky asserted that social and cultural forces are the predominant influence on human development. Vygotsky is famous for the so-called socio-cultural cognitive theory, which identifies language as the fundamental driver of reason and memory. Moreover, adherents to this theory believe that an individual's social milieu exerts major influence on his thought processes. The society in which one develops suggests the form and content of both intellectual development and expression. For this reason, Vygotsky asserted that learning should be focused on the acquisition of cultural artifacts, like language, mnemonics, and mathematics.

Lifespan perspective

Unlike other approaches to developmental psychology, which often indicate that development ends during adulthood, the lifespan perspective emphasizes continuous progress until death. This perspective also suggests that development occurs in several dimensions: biology, intellect, attention, abstract thinking, and social skill. Development is multi-directional, according to this perspective. In other words, age and experience cause changes in all sorts of fields. The degree to which a person can change is called his plasticity of development. The lifespan perspective emphasizes that development occurs within the context of a person's family, community, religion, peer group, and society.

lifespan - several dimensions
1. biology
2. intellect
3. attention
4. abstract thinking
5. social skill

Research Strategies and Methodology

Case study

In the case study method of data gathering, research focuses on a single person rather than on a collection of people. This is a form of longitudinal design, in which one subject is isolated, and often one special aspect of that person's life is studied in close detail. Of course, the results of a case study do not provide comparisons with other people. It is common for case studies to be tainted by the prejudices of the researcher, so results should be carefully studied before being accepted as valid.

Limitations

The most obvious problem with the case study approach to data gathering is that it isolates one person, and therefore cannot make descriptions about a population at large. Another potential problem is that over the course of the study the subject and the researcher will become so familiar that their relationship will taint the results of the study. For instance, the researcher may develop a positive or negative opinion about the subject, which may prejudice his research. It is very useful for case studies to involve a strict protocol and multiple researchers to guard against creeping bias by a particular individual.

Correlational research

Like descriptive research, correlational research is distinct from experimental research. Whereas descriptive research is mainly restricted to observation and record-keeping, correlational research aims at diagnosing the causal relationships between environment and behavior. For instance, a correlational research study might examine a link between caffeine consumption and aggressive behavior. As with descriptive research, correlational research issues intervention in the lives of the subject. However, the results of correlational research cannot be said to firmly establish causal relationships, as a broad array of factors can contribute to a specific behavior.

Correlational analysis

Correlational analysis is used to draw links between the variables observed during a research study. It should be noted, however, that correlational analysis does not establish causal relationships between variables. In correlational analysis, numerical data is placed on a graph. The degree to which the variables correlate is known as the correlation coefficient. A correlational coefficient can range from -1.00, a perfect negative correlation, to +1.00, a perfect positive correlation. A perfect negative correlation means that when one variable occurs, the other variable never occurs. A perfect positive correlation means that when one variable occurs, the other variable always occurs as well.

Cross-sectional design   *Cross-sectional - diff age groups*

Cross-sectional design is a form of research study in which the members of several different age groups are examined simultaneously. Usually, this type of study is performed to identify differences between people of various ages. For instance, an experiment might be aimed at identifying differences in memory between twenty-year-olds and fifty-year-olds. A cross-sectional design study can yield some of the same benefits as a longitudinal design study because it includes subjects of all different ages. In addition, it only requires one sampling session, and is therefore much easier to perform. Of course, this study does not allow researchers to use the same individuals over a long interval.

Disadvantages

The main disadvantage of cross-sectional research is that it is extremely hard to find subject groups appropriate for comparison. Even a slight age difference can have a significant effect on the results, as the economic, social, and political trends in the country can exercise vastly different influences on the members of the population who are of a different age. The reactions to given external forces may be completely different for individuals of different generations. These differences related to age and background can sometimes make it difficult to isolate trends in cross-sectional design data. Indeed, this phenomenon of confusion is so common it has been given a name: confounding.

Sequential design *sequential → longitudinal + cross-sectional*

Sequential design research is a sort of combination of the longitudinal and cross-sectional designs. In this design study, multiple age groups are evaluated over an interval. Sometimes, this interval is very long, like five or ten years. A sequential design study, then, both examines the same individuals over time and simultaneously compares individuals of different ages. These studies are not vulnerable to the singular events, as for instance major wars, that can affect longitudinal studies. Usually, a sequential design study can be viewed in terms of its longitudinal or cross-sectional data.

Experimental design

In an experimental design, the avowed purpose of the research is to answer a particular question. Generally, the question has to do with the effects of making a particular change or adjustment to a single variable. Experimental design research is the best way to diagnose causal relationships between variables. The independent variable is the factor manipulated by researchers, while the dependent variable is not adjusted intentionally. Experimental design research produces clear and easy-to-assess findings, but is perhaps more limited in its scope than other forms of research.

Limitations

One problem with experimental design is that certain variables, such as age, socioeconomic background, and health, are inextricable from the behavior of the subject but cannot be adjusted by the researcher. These are known as extraneous variables, and they can have a great deal of influence on the results of experimental research. Another potential problem with experimental design is that it can be hazardous or unethical; some questions or inquiries are seen as offensive by certain ethnic groups. Some researchers claim that there is a clear observation bias in experimental research. In other words, subjects perform differently in the context of an experiment than they would in real life. Also, experiments can be extremely expensive and time-intensive.

Longitudinal design

[handwritten: longitudenel - subject over long period of time or lifespan]

Longitudinal design requires that subjects be monitored over an extremely long interval, often their entire lives. For instance, subjects of a longitudinal study may be interviewed every ten years. These experiments can be very difficult to develop and maintain, but they yield results that are unobtainable by any other method. Longitudinal studies can show lifelong progress, and can deliver fascinating insights about health, personal development, and social relationships over the long term. In order to get a full picture of human development, psychologists must continue to produce longitudinal studies.

Disadvantages
Longitudinal studies have significant design flaws, not the least of which is the fact that the members of the subject group will change markedly over such a long interval. In some cases, the members of the group will move far away or die, making it difficult to keep up with them. Sometimes, the members of a longitudinal study will lose interest or decide they no longer want to participate, which leaves researchers with a great deal of wasted time and energy. Similarly, there can be changes in motivation and competence among the researchers; it is unlikely that the same group of scientists will administer the study from beginning to end. Some longitudinal studies run into funding problems, while others discover partway through that there are significant flaws in the methods or content of questioning. It is very difficult to make positive adjustments to a longitudinal study once it has begun.

Descriptive research

Descriptive research is a bit more free-form than experimental research; it entails the observation and recording of behavior. Descriptive research works best when it is aimed at identifying the instances of a particular action or type of action, such as aggressive behavior. Information for descriptive research can be obtained through observation, standardized tests, interviews, surveys, or case studies. In this type of research, the observer does not influence the behavior of the subject in any way. In other words, there is no manipulated variable. Descriptive research is not concerned with the causes of behavior, but simply with recording its appearances.

Social survey

Social survey method of data collection, researchers take a look at the beliefs and behaviors of a large number of people. However, researchers do not individually question each member of the group. Instead, they draw a random sample of Representative members and question them. Information may be obtained from the sample group through face-to-face interviews, online questionnaires, or surveys sent through the mail. The results of social surveys can be valuable, so long as it can be assured that the responding group is representative of the population at large. Also, the survey instrument must have clear, comprehensible questions that produce easy to measure answers.

Disadvantages
Social surveys must overcome internal biases and a lack of responses. The surveys depend on the voluntary participation of subjects, which is often not forthcoming. Moreover, there may be significant differences between those who respond to a survey and those who do not, and these differences can call into question the validity of the study. When social

surveys gather information through interviews, it is quite possible that the subjects will adjust their responses depending on the personality and perceived interests of the researcher. In other words, the subject of an interview is likely to conform his answers to what he believes the researcher wants. Some people lie during interviews, and other people are unwilling to discuss personal matters candidly. Finally, social surveys are almost impossible to use with infants and young children.

Naturalistic observation

Naturalistic observation is a technique for data collection in which researchers closely monitor the behavior of people in their normal, everyday environment. Perhaps the most common example of naturalistic observation occurs in schools, when administrators unobtrusively sit in on a class to observe teacher and student behavior. In some cases, the observer may record observations with a notepad, tape recorder, or video camera. It is important that the observer have access to basic information about the subjects, such as their ages and backgrounds. Typically, naturalistic observation is a part of descriptive research.

Limitations

Naturalistic observation tends to be only as good as the environment in which it is conducted. Since there is no manipulation of the environment, as there is in experimental research, all of the observations must be made with the caveat that total environmental control was not attempted. For this reason, there is always the possibility that unseen or unacknowledged factors are influencing behavior. Also, naturalistic observation tends to be weakened when the observer has specific biases or intentions in observation. Sometimes, observers merely see what they want to see. Finally, the subjects of naturalistic observation may alter their behavior because they know they are being observed.

Cross-cultural studies

Cross-cultural studies are used to determine the validity of theories for more than one society. Sometimes, things that are true of one society are not true of another. The range of influences and cultural artifacts in one setting may vastly alter behavior and beliefs. To determine whether theories about one culture can be applied to another, researchers isolate a particular variable in two cultures and compare its appearances. For instance, in Hispanic culture there is often more loyalty to the matriarch than the patriarch. This has specific effects on child psychology, which can be studied and then compared with observations from other cultures.

Limitations

Cross-cultural studies require money and travel, so it is common for much of the data to be collected by amateurs and untrained researchers. This means that the quality of the data is variable. In some cultures, there may be very little background information, and so researchers must basically start from scratch. Cross-cultural studies often over-generalize about foreign cultures, ignoring the differences between individual members of the group. Also, researchers who conduct cross-cultural studies must guard against overemphasizing their own cultural perspective. For instance, it has long been a contention of third-world citizens that their lives are seen only through the lens of American and Western European thought.

Standardized tests in developmental research

Developmental researchers often use standardized tests, which are assessments with established questions and procedures for administration. Standardized tests are valuable because they can be replicated with different people and in different settings. At this point, the most effective standardized tests are those used to assess intelligence and personality. Of course, no standardized test is able to account for fluctuations in mood and motivation by the test-taker. Human behavior is unstable and inconsistent, which can weaken the validity of standardized testing.

Population and sample

In the context of research, a population is the whole group being studied. Typically, the size of the population will be defined by the parameters of the study. The population could be the citizens of a town, the members of a high school class, or the attendees of a certain church. However large or small, the population must be strictly defined in order for the research to be useful. Sometimes, it is impractical for an entire population to be studied, and so researchers will select a representative portion of the population, known as a sample. Samples can be chosen at random, but it is better for researchers to use established method of sampling. It is very important that the method of sampling be capable of extracting a representative selection of people.

Time sampling and event sampling

Time sampling and event sampling are techniques by which an observer can guarantee objectivity in naturalistic studies. These are methods of assuring symmetry in observation. In time sampling, the observer selects a particular interval, and then counts the instances of the target behavior during that interval. For example, the observer might decide to count instances over ten minute spans for each of the subjects. In event sampling, the observer reports the duration of each instance of the target behavior. Every time the behavior occurs, the observer uses a clock or stopwatch to measure how long it goes on.

Cohort effects

All of the influences on the development of a person that have to do with the era in which he lives are known as cohort effects. For example, children of the Great Depression are likely to exhibit different behaviors towards money and financial responsibility than are children of the 1990s, a period of relative prosperity. The mores and attitudes of a society change over time, and the citizens of the population are likely to receive different opportunities and messages from the community depending on when they were born. Researchers must pay particular attention to cohort effects when examining the effects of age on subjects; sometimes, what is believed to be an idiosyncrasy or a personality characteristic is actually a response to environmental stimuli.

Ethics in developmental research

Gathering data about people may be the primary intention of researchers, but it is also necessary to guard the rights and privacy of subjects. The subject of a research project should never run the risk of physical or mental harm. For this reason, university-funded or -operated projects typically have to be approved by an ethics committee, and professional organizations like the American Psychological Association and Society for Research in Child Development have strict guidelines for research in their fields. There are requirements for consent and confidentiality. The subjects of a research study must be given sufficient information about the purpose of the study and the methods to be used.

Confidentiality in research

All those people who participate in a study have a right to privacy and confidentiality. In most studies, the data is recorded and reported in such a way that it is impossible to ascertain the identity of the subject. Also, the information collected by the researcher should remain confidential as much as possible. The only scenario in which a researcher has the right to divulge confidential information is if it has the potential to affect the safety of the subject or others. In order to divulge specific information related to individual performance, the researcher needs to obtain permission from the subject.

Informed consent and deception in research

In research, subjects have the right to be told about the purpose, methodology, and potential risks of participation. There are established requirements related to informed consent, meaning that participants have the right to obtain whatever information they want before they assent. Also, subjects have the right to end their participation at any time. Of course, in some situations the research will be invalidated if the participants are fully informed ahead of time. When this is the case, it is the responsibility of the researcher to ensure that this deception will not harm the participants, and that all of the information justifying this deception is made available to participants upon completion of the study.

Biological Development Throughout the Life Span

Brain

There are three main structures in the brain: the cerebrum, the cerebellum, and the brain stem. The cerebrum makes up about 85% of the brain's weight, and is divided into left and right hemispheres. Each of these hemispheres has four lobes: frontal, occipital, temporal, and parietal. The frontal lobes control processes like cognition, intentional motion, and planning. The occipital lobes are mainly concerned with vision. The temporal lobes manage functions like audition, language production, and memory. The parietal lobes are related to motor functions, spatial orientation, and concentration. The cerebellum is mainly devoted to posture, physical orientation, and balance. Finally, the brainstem controls the most basic functions of the body, like breathing and circulation.

Nervous system

The nervous system controls the functions of the body, and collects information about body processes. It has a few components. The central nervous system consists of the brain and spinal cord. The central nervous system compiles information about the external and internal environment and generates responses to these stimuli. The information acted upon by the central nervous system is collected by the peripheral nervous system. Information is transmitted to the spinal cord and brain through 12 pairs of cranial nerves and 31 pairs of spinal nerves. All of the body functions that are not under conscious control, as for instance respiration and digestion, are controlled by the autonomic nervous system.

Brain development

Prenatal
About 2 ½ weeks after fertilization, the brain and central nervous system of the infant begin to develop. The first step is the emergence of a neural tube, which is a long, hollow structure along the dorsal side of the embryo. The top of this tube closes off about 25 days after conception, and the lower end closes off two days later. At the top end of the tube, a brain will develop. About five weeks after fertilization, nerve cells, also known as neurons, will begin to proliferate. Approximately 23 weeks into the pregnancy, connections between these neurons will be formed.

Early childhood
During the first years of childhood, the nervous system and brain develop rapidly. In part, this is because the infant is experiencing a wealth of novel sensations. As the brain and nervous system develop, there are more connections between axons and dendrites, and there is additional myelin on the outside of axons. In other words, the synaptic connections in the brain and nervous system are faster and more numerous. Also, in early childhood the brain gets better at communicating with itself. There is particular progress made in the frontal cortex, which is associated with higher-level functions like planning and problem-solving. Amazingly, a five-year-old will have already obtained approximately 90% of his adult brain weight.

Middle childhood

In middle childhood, the brain and nervous system continue to develop properly, so long as the child receives sufficient sleep and nutrition. However, malnutrition, a lack of sensory stimulation, abuse, or a dangerous home life can impede the progress of development. During middle childhood, as the child passes through elementary school, his cognition will improve in terms of speed, volume, and efficiency. Memory makes significant progress during this period, and the child develops the ability to reason abstractly and solve complicated problems.

Brain function

Midlife

In midlife, or between the ages of 45 and 65, the brain and nervous system begin to slow a bit. People at this age will have more crystallized, or permanent knowledge, but will have less intellectual agility and deftness. It may take a person in this stage of life a bit longer to solve a new problem. Nevertheless, a person in midlife will have more experience dealing with different situations, and will be able to apply knowledge more broadly. During midlife, the memory may begin to diminish, as the prefrontal cortex atrophies. However, people who remain intellectually active tend to lose fewer brain cells.

Older adults

Over the span from age 20 to 90, a person will lose between 5 and 10% of brain weight. Moreover, the brain will decrease during this interval by 15% in volume. Some scientists believe that this decrease is caused by the elimination of dendrites, damage to the myelin sheaths on axons, or to the deaths of brain cells. However, none of these theories have been conclusively proved. As the brain shrinks, the individual will experience memory and cognitive deficits. Also, older adults tend to have diminished reflexes and physical coordination.

Cephalocaudal and proximodistal principles of development

Human physical development can be described as occurring according to either the cephalocaudal or proximodistal principles. In the cephalocaudal model, human development starts in the head, and specifically the brain, and moves down through the torso into the lower extremities. This model aligns with the development of the fetus and young child. In particular, the nervous system's development seems to begin with the brain stem and proceed downward. The proximodistal model, on the other hand, describes growth as progressing from a central axis, the spinal column, outward to the extremities. This model of growth is consistent with the superiority of strength in the core of the body, and the necessity of developing central muscular systems before peripheral ones.

Genes and chromosomes

The fundamental unit of heredity is the gene, a tiny part of the cell that communicates information about development to the body. Genes are passed on from parent to child. A gene is a short part of the DNA molecule found in the nucleus of every cell. Among the functions stimulated by genes are cell reproduction and protein synthesis. Chromosomes, meanwhile, are tiny, thread-like structures composed of DNA and found in the nuclei of cells. A human fetus has 23 pairs, composed in equal parts of genetic material from the mother and father.

Dominant and recessive genes

Human beings inherit genes from each parent for certain characteristics. For instance, a baby will have the genes related to hair color from both his mother and his father. When one of the genes is dominant, it overpowers the other gene and manifests in the child's development. The gene that is overpowered is called the recessive gene. Recessive genes may contribute to development if they are reinforced by another recessive gene in the same pair. However, if the child has one recessive gene and one dominant gene in a particular chromosome, the dominant gene will always win out.

Genetic counseling

When an individual or a couple discovers a family history of genetic disease or abnormality, they may consult with a genetic counselor to determine the likelihood of passing this condition on to their offspring. Many people do not want to have a child if they feel there is a strong likelihood that the child will be severely handicapped. In addition, it can be very expensive and time-consuming to care for a handicapped child. A genetic counselor can provide information to couples so that they can make a more educated decision about reproduction. Sometimes, genetic counselors are asked to consult with couples who do not have particular genetic disorders in their history, but are simply advanced in age.

Puberty and hormones

Hormones are the chemicals that motivate the body to do certain things. They are produced in the organs that make up the endocrine system. With the exception of the sex organs, males and females have identical endocrine systems. The actions of the hormones are determined by the hypothalamus, an area of the brain about the size of a pea. The hypothalamus sends messages to the pituitary gland, which is directly beneath it. The pituitary gland turns on and off the various glands that produce hormones. Hormones, once released, are carried to their targets by the blood stream, at which point they motivate cells and organs to action. Hormones can influence the way a person looks, feels, behaves, or matures.

The sex hormones that are most important to women are called estrogen and progesterone and are produced in the ovaries. In males, the primary sex hormone is testosterone, which is produced by the adrenal glands and testes. Both men and women do, however, have small amounts of the opposite hormone. Indeed, men need estrogen to have effective sperm. Sex hormones are at work very early in the development of the embryo. When testes are formed, they begin releasing testosterone, which causes the formation of the other male reproductive parts, like the penis. If no testosterone is present, the embryo will develop female genitals. This is true of both natural females and males with malfunctioning testes.

Effects of drug use

The effects of habitual drug use can be either chronic (resulting from long-term use) or acute (resulting from a single dose). Acute effects are usually determined by the particular drug; first-time users of stimulants, for instance, may be overcome with a powerful sense of anger. The effects of chronic drug use are more predictable. Over a long period of time,

- 17 -

consistent drug users may feel tired, lose weight, have a nagging cough, and develop overall body aches. Drug abusers often suffer from blackouts and may undergo psychological turmoil and bouts of paranoia. Typically, the stress involved with supporting and maintaining a habit increases over time, and this stress adds to the damage done by the drug itself.

Learning and behavior

Understanding how learning and behavior work in the reward circuit can help understand the action of addictive drugs. Drug addiction is characterized by strong, drug seeking behaviors in which the addict persistently craves and seeks out drugs, despite the knowledge of harmful consequences. Addictive drugs produce a reward, which is the euphoric feeling resulting from sustained DA concentrations in the synaptic cleft of neurons in the brain. Operant conditioning is exhibited in drug addicts as well as laboratory mice, rats, and primates; they are able to associate an action or behavior, in this case seeking out the drug, with a reward, which is the effect of the drug. Evidence shows that this behavior is most likely a result of the synaptic changes which have occurred due to repeated drug exposure. The drug seeking behavior is induced by glutamatergic projections from the prefrontal cortex to the NAc. This idea is supported with data from experiments showing the drug seeking behavior can be prevented following the inhibition of AMPA glutamate receptors and glutamate release in the NAc.

Brain damage in teens

Early drug use is linked to later depression in teen girls, but in boys the study found no evidence that drug use leads to depression, or that depression leads to drug use. Young drug abusers are up to three times more likely to suffer brain damage than those who do not use drugs. Scientists at the University of Edinburgh studied the brains of 34 deceased intravenous drug abusers of heroin and methadone and compared them to the brains of 16 young people who were not drug users. Their examination revealed brain damage in the drug abusers normally seen in much older people. The damaged nerve cells were in the areas of the brain involved in learning, memory and emotional well being, and were similar to damage found in the early stages of Alzheimer's disease. The study showed evidence of an increased risk of brain damage associated with heroin and methadone use, which may be highest in the young, when individuals are most likely to acquire the habit. It was found that the brains of these young drug abusers showed significantly higher levels of two key proteins associated with brain damage. In a previous study it was found that drug abuse causes low grade inflammation in the brain. Taken together, the two studies suggest that intravenous opiate abuse may be linked to premature aging of the brain. The drug abusers who were examined in the study sadly died at a young age, but there are many others who do not realize the long-term effects that these drugs may be causing.

Neuroplasticity in early drug use

Neuroplasticity is the putative mechanism behind learning and memory. It involves physical changes in the synapses between two communicating neurons, characterized by increased gene expression, altered cell signaling, and the formation of new synapses between the communicating neurons. When addictive drugs are present in the system, they appear to hijack this mechanism in the reward system so that motivation is geared towards procuring the drug rather than natural rewards. Depending on the history of drug use, nucleus accumbens (NAc) excitatory synapses experience two types of neuroplasticity, or bidirectional plasticity, long-term potentiation (LTP) and long-term depression (LTD). It has been displayed that chronic exposure to cocaine increases the strength of synapses in NAc

- 18 -

after a 10-14 day withdrawal period, while strengthened synapses did not appear within a 24 hour withdrawal period after repeated cocaine exposure. A single dose of cocaine did not display any attributes of a strengthened synapse. When drug experienced subjects were challenged with one dose of cocaine, synaptic depression occurred. Therefore, it seems the history of cocaine exposure along with withdrawal times affects the direction of glutamatergic plasticity in the NAc

Decreased neurogenesis
Drug addiction also raises the issue of potential harmful effects on the development of new neurons in adults. Eisch and Harburg raise three new concepts they have extrapolated from the numerous recent studies on drug addiction. First, neurogenesis decreases as a result of repeated exposure to additive drugs. A list of studies show that chronic use of opiates, psychostimulants, nicotine, and alcohol decrease neurogenesis. Second, this apparent decrease in neurogenesis seems to be independent of HPA axis activation. Other environmental factors other than drug exposure such as age, stress and exercise, can also have an effect of neurogenesis by regulating the hypothalamic-pituitary-adrenal (HPA) axis. Mounting evidence suggests this for 3 reasons: small doses of opiates and psychostimulants increase corticosterone concentration in serum but with no effect of neurogenesis; although decreased neurogenesis is similar between self-administered and forced drug intake, activation of HPA axis is greater in self-administration subjects; and even after the inhibition of opiate induced increase of corticosterone, a decrease in neurogenesis occurred. Last, addictive drugs appear to only affect proliferation in the subgranular zone (SGZ), rather than other areas associated with neurogenesis. The studies of drug use and neurogenesis may have implications on stem cell biology

Gross vs. fine motor skills

Physiologists make a distinction between gross motor skills, which require large muscle groups, and fine motor skills, which require the use of small muscle groups, like those on the fingers and hands. Some examples of gross motor skills are standing, kicking, walking, running, crawling, and throwing. Fine motor skills are exemplified by actions like typing, sewing, sign language, and drawing. It takes a person much longer to develop fine motor skills than gross motor skills. Many of the important day-to-day activities require fine motor skills, however. For instance, putting on clothes and tying shoes require intricate movements by the fingers. Of course, most activities require a combination of fine and gross motor skills.

Motor skill development

Two-year olds
The second year after birth is marked by rapid progress in motor skills. In the 15th month after birth, a child will often be able to walk by himself. By the end of the 24th month, that same child will be able to run and jump forward about one foot in distance. A two-year-old should be able to drag a toy, walk backwards, kick and throw a ball, and balance in a squatting position. The child at this age should be able to ascend and descend stairs on his hands and knees. The two-year-old should be able to turn the pages in a book, hold a plastic cup, and stack blocks.

Ages three to five

At three years of age, a child should be able to catch a ball, run, jump, hop, and ride a tricycle or big wheel. At this point, fine motor skills will have developed as well, and the child should be able to draw a reasonably straight line and copy a circle. By the age of four years, the child should be able to gallop, put on clothes, and navigate complicated play equipment, like a jungle gym. As for fine motor skills, a four-year-old should be able to cut with scissors and replicate letters and numbers on paper. At five years, the child should be able to hop on one foot, sprint, and skip. A five-year-old should be able to copy all the basic symbols and shapes.

Middle childhood years

Entering middle childhood, the rate of motor skill development slows down. Middle childhood, which runs from about five to fourteen years of age, is marked by the gradual refinement of basic gross and fine motor skills. During these years, the child will become more coordinated and in control of his body. A child at this age should be able to learn games like baseball and basketball, and should be able to master riding a bike or a skateboard. During middle childhood, endurance and intensity of effort increase, and there are significantly fewer differences between boys and girls then there will be later in life.

Learning to walk

It is typical for a child in the United States to begin walking between 11 and 15 months after birth. The development of walking requires a number of fundamental gross motor skills, like raising the head, rolling over, and sitting without support. The muscles of the legs and torso must be sufficiently developed to hold the child upright. A child typically begins to walk by pulling herself up into a standing position, and then walking with some assistance. For many children, the process starts with crawling, then creeping, and finally standing upright before walking. However, some children skip one of these steps. Walking requires enough strength to balance on one leg briefly while stepping forward with the other.

Development of manual skills

Two months after birth, an infant will be able to move his arms and upper body toward an object, but he will not be able to clutch it. Three months after birth, the infant will be able to incorporate shoulder and elbow into his movement, though he still will be swiping with a closed fist. A month later, the child will be able to use an open hand to grasp an object, and approximately five months after birth, the child will be able to gently touch the object. There may be some semblance of a grip at this stage, though for most children a recognizable grip does not develop until about 36 weeks after birth. At first, a child is likely to put objects into his mouth. After about two years of development, infants should be able to hold and use a writing utensil, a fork or spoon, and a toothbrush.

Food pyramid

The United States Department of Agriculture created the food pyramid to illustrate the composition of a healthy diet. On the food pyramid, foods are arranged into four levels, depending on the volume in which they should be consumed. Grains are on the bottom level. Included in this category are bread, rice, pasta, and cereal. On the second level are fruits and vegetables. This means that a person should consume slightly more grains than fruits or vegetables. Above the fruits and vegetables are two groups, the meats and the dairy. Meats include eggs, nuts, fish, and dry beans. The dairy group includes cheese, milk, and yogurt. The top of the pyramid is made up of fats, oils, and sweets. The tip of the pyramid is very small, indicating that a person should not consume very many foods from this category.

Nutritional importance of vitamin C

Vitamin C, also known as ascorbic acid, is important because it helps protect the health of the skin, bones, teeth, cartilage, and blood vessels.
- Vitamin C protects these areas of the body primarily by acting as an antioxidant that helps reduce the negative effects that oxygen reactions within the body can have on the cells.
- Vitamin C is also necessary in the production of collagen, which is a protein necessary for skin and cartilage health.
- Significant vitamin C deficiencies can result in a number of serious health problems including a disorder known as scurvy, in which the body lacks the collagen it requires to maintain the health of the skin. Scurvy ultimately leads to the formation of liver spots on the skin and gums, and can also cause bleeding from all the body's mucous membranes including the nose, lips, ears, and other areas.
- Common sources of vitamin C include strawberries, oranges, lemons, limes, mangos, grapes, broccoli, potatoes, spinach, liver, and milk.

Nutritional importance of Vitamin E

Vitamin E, also known as tocopherol, is important primarily because it aids in maintaining proper brain function and eye health.
- It has also been suggested that vitamin E may help reduce the risk of cancer, cataracts, heart disease, and other health conditions as well as helping treat patients that have Parkinson's or Alzheimer's Disease.
- A significant vitamin E deficiency can result in muscle weakness, blindness, and neurological problems as a result of the body transmitting nerve impulses incorrectly.
- Common sources of vitamin E include peanuts, hazelnuts, coconuts, corn, asparagus, carrots, tomatoes, fish, peanut butter, and vegetable oils.
- There are also many multivitamins and supplements that supply vitamin E, but some studies have shown that some synthetic vitamins and supplements may actually be significantly less beneficial or even have a negative impact on the individual when taken in large doses.
- Both men and women do require vitamin E, in similar amounts, to continue functioning normally.

Nutritional importance of fiber

Fiber is an important part of an individual's diet because it helps with bowel movements, digestion, and immune responses.
- Fiber has also been shown to lower blood cholesterol, help prevent obesity, lower the risk of certain types of cancer including colon cancer, and lower the risk of type 2 diabetes.

- A significant lack of fiber in an individual's diet can lead to symptoms such as constipation and slower digestion and can cause an individual to have a higher risk of developing certain diseases.
- Some common sources of fiber include certain breakfast cereals, oatmeal, whole-wheat bread, beans, apples, pears, strawberries, bananas, potatoes, onions, and green beans.
- Both men and women require similar amounts of fiber to continue functioning properly.

Nutritional importance of vitamin B12

B12, also known as cyanocobalamin, is important because it is necessary for the production of blood cells and aids in maintaining the health of the nervous system.
- A severe lack of B12 within the body can lead to a variety of conditions including megaloblastic anemia, a condition in which the red blood cells have less hemoglobin and therefore have more difficulty functioning properly.
- A significant lack of B12 can also lead to severe problems with the nervous system because the lack of B12 causes the disintegration and death of nerve cells.
- Individuals who lack significant quantities of B12 may develop symptoms such as numbness, tingling, and difficulty with muscle control.
- Some common sources of B12 include chicken, beef, pork, liver, fish, shellfish, certain breakfast cereals, milk, cheese, eggs, and yogurt.
- Vegetarians may have difficulty getting enough B12 since the primary sources of B12 are meat products, but B12 supplements and multivitamins can be a good option as well.

Nutritional importance of protein

Protein is important to the functioning of a healthy individual because it is necessary for the body to produce the amino acids it needs to continue functioning.
- Most of the amino acids that the body needs are already present in the body, but certain amino acids, known as essential amino acids, can only be produced when the body digests protein.
- A severe lack of protein is usually caused by malnutrition and can lead to reduced brain function, intellectual disabilities, and an overall weakening of the immune system due to a decrease in the number of white blood cells.
- It has also been suggested that a significant lack of protein may lead to conditions such as kwashiokor, which causes significant weight loss, thinning and discolored hair, swelling of the organs, and weakens the responses of the immune system.
- Some common sources of protein include chicken, beef, wheat, rice, milk, cheese, eggs, peas, beans, peanuts, and peanut butter.

Obesity

In simple terms, a person puts on weight when he consumes more calories than he burns. It is easier to overconsume when eating foods high in fat and sugar, since these foods contain more calories than do fruits and vegetables. In the United States, many individuals develop poor dietary habits during childhood, and these habits contribute to the development of obesity later in life. A sedentary lifestyle, with a great deal of time in front of a computer or television screen, often leads to obesity. Of course, many people have a hereditary disposition towards obesity, and may have to strive throughout life to overcome this genetic inclination. Also, research has suggested that low socioeconomic status is correlated with obesity.

Malnutrition

A person can develop malnutrition if he eats a bad diet or has a physiological inability to absorb and use certain nutrients. Interestingly, doctors also define overconsumption of food as malnutrition. In other words, an obese person can be as poorly nourished as an emaciated person. Malnutrition can be caused by a general lack of calories, or a specific lack of protein, vitamins, or minerals. Epidemics of malnutrition are often related to natural disasters, war, and extremely bad economic conditions. Moreover, individuals who know very little about nutrition are more likely to become malnourished. Some of the diseases related to malnutrition and include anemia, caused by low levels of iron or copper; kwashiorkor, associated with low levels of protein; and marasmus, associated with the general low calorie consumption.

Divisions of the prenatal period

Biologists isolate three divisions in the prenatal period of infant development: the germinal period, the embryonic period, and the fetal period. The germinal period, which consists of the first two weeks after conception, is initiated by the fertilization of the egg and concludes with the zygote affixing itself to the uterine wall. During the embryonic period, which lasts from the end of the germinal period to about the eighth week of pregnancy, the major organs begin to develop and the body takes on a recognizably human appearance. In the final period, the fetal, the body becomes viable. The fetal period runs from about the ninth week until the end of the pregnancy.

Prenatal development

Germinal period
The germinal period of pregnancy lasts for two weeks after fertilization. In the first week, the zygote moves from the fallopian tubes into the uterus and attaches to the wall there. At this point, cell division through mitosis has already begun. In mitosis, a cell splits apart into two other cells with the same chromosomes and genes as the original cell. At the end of the germinal period, there will be enough cells for the inner cell mass of the blastocyst to have three distinct layers proceeding from outside to inside: the ectoderm, which will become the sense organs, skin, and nervous system; the mesoderm which will become the circulatory system, bones, kidneys, and muscles; and the endoderm, which will become the bladder, respiratory system, digestive system, and part of the reproductive system.

Embryonic period
During the embryonic period, it becomes possible to see that the embryo is a human fetus. The embryonic period runs from the third to the eighth week of pregnancy. At this point, both cephalocaudal and proximodistal development are in full swing. Cephalocaudal development begins in the head and moves down through the body, while proximodistal development is the growth of tissue on the left and right sides of what is known as the primitive streak, the early stages of spinal cord development.

Fetal period
The final period of prenatal development, known as the fetal period, extends from about the ninth week of pregnancy to birth. The embryo is now known as a fetus, with a face, internal organs, and appendages. The fetus will even have fingers and toes. After about 20 weeks of gestation, the fetus will be approximately one foot long and will have a heartbeat that can be heard with a stethoscope. Four or five weeks later, the fetus will be sufficiently developed to survive outside the womb, though it is likely that such an early baby would require respiratory assistance.

Puberty

Puberty is the set of physical changes that shift a person from childhood into adulthood. The age at which a person begins puberty varies widely. Girls tend to enter puberty before boys. A girl may begin to develop breasts and pubic hair at age 9, while a boy will not experience any genital growth until at least age 10. Menstruation typically begins around age 11 or 12 for girls, but it may occur as late as 15. For some people, puberty only lasts a year and a half, though it can last up to five years.

Physical changes
One of the most immediately apparent changes caused by puberty is a rapid growth in height and weight. Girls typically begin this growth spurt about two years earlier than boys. In the midst of this growth spurt, however, a girl may grow 3 ½ inches each year, while a boy can grow up to 4 inches annually. During puberty, both boys and girls will begin to develop pubic and underarm hair. Girls will experience breast development, and will begin to menstruate. The first menstruation is called menarche. During puberty, the hips of the female will expand, while the male will develop more musculature and facial hair. Males will also experience a deepening of the voice.

Endocrine system
During puberty, the endocrine system will stimulate changes by producing a different cocktail of hormones. In particular, hormones associated with puberty are produced by the hypothalamus, gonads, and pituitary gland. The hypothalamus is located in the brain, where it manages the sympathetic nervous system, coordinates the nervous and endocrine systems, and maintains a steady body temperature (a process known as homeostasis). The pituitary gland monitors other glands and regulates the overall growth of the body. Gonads are often considered to be synonymous with the male testes, though the female ovaries are gonads as well. Gonads produce testosterone and estradiol, which is a form of estrogen directly linked with puberty.

Emerging adulthood

Dr. Jeffrey Arnett, in a 2000 article in American Psychologist, defined emerging adulthood as a period of development between ages 18 and 29, during which a person focuses on developing their adult persona and choosing a career and lifestyle. Emerging adults have five characteristics in common. They are actively working to develop an identity, in part by finding a vocation. They live unstable lifestyles, frequently moving and changing jobs. They are primarily focused on themselves. They feel as if they are in between stages of life. Finally, emerging adults are generally optimistic about their future.

Physical peak of performance

For most people, peak physical performance occurs between the ages of 20 and 30. A female reaches her maximum height at age 20, while a male may continue to grow until age 30. By the age of 35, both men and women will have achieved peak bone mass and muscular endurance. The heart and lungs seem to perform best during the 20s, after which point the body begins a slow decline. The tone and strength of muscle diminishes, fatty tissue increases, and the lens loses some ability to register focus and shade. Also, hearing begins to diminish around the age of 30.

Health issues of emerging and early adulthood

Emerging adults tend to be quite healthy, but they may be developing habits of behavior that will cause problems later in life. For instance, many emerging adults smoke, drink too much, sleep too little, exercise infrequently, and eat bad foods. Also, emerging adults may not take care of their reproductive health, and may not have access to basic health care services. Substance addiction and sexually transmitted diseases are especially common among emerging adults. Interestingly, according to the Berkeley Longitudinal Study, a strong predictor of life satisfaction at age 70 is when an individual at age 30 receives help to overcome these health issues.

Middle adulthood

The precise range of middle adulthood is disputed. Although the numerical midpoint of life is about 39, most Americans consider middle age or middle adulthood to be between 40 and 65. During middle age, a body begins to lose some of its efficiency, and the sensory organs decline in function. Men tend to endure more significant drop-offs than women, and indeed more men die during middle age than do women. In particular, people with African ancestry seem to be prone to significant health problems during middle age.

Physical changes common in middle adulthood

In middle adulthood, most people undergo subtle but significant physical changes. The skin will begin to wrinkle, sag, and may develop some age spots. The hair will turn gray and become thinner. Many men go bald during middle adulthood. Height will diminish slightly, and weight is likely to increase. In particular, middle-aged people tend to put on fat. At the same time, people over the age of 50 lose muscle tone, and thereby strength. This is particularly true in the legs and the back. Around this time, the tendons of the ligaments lose their elasticity, and the person is more likely to suffer from joint stiffness. Women are susceptible to osteoporosis during middle adulthood, and both men and women must be on the lookout for high blood pressure, arthritis, and diabetes.

Cholesterol

High cholesterol and high blood pressure, otherwise known as hypertension, are problems often faced by middle-aged adults. There are two kinds of cholesterol: high-density lipoprotein (HDL, also known as good cholesterol) and low-density lipoprotein (LDL, also known as bad cholesterol). Some cholesterol is necessary, but if there is too much low-density lipoprotein in the bloodstream, it can build up the on the walls of the arteries and cause hardening, a condition known as atherosclerosis. Individuals with elevated levels of high-density lipoprotein and low levels of low-density lipoprotein have a reduced risk of cardiovascular disease.

Presbyopia

Presbyopia is an aging-related eye condition in which the lens hardens and the eye loses the ability to focus closely. This condition typically sets in around age 40. A person who suffers from presbyopia is likely to have a hard time reading small print or working on a computer. He is likely to prefer reading type from a distance of several feet. Bifocals, contact lenses, or half-glasses can be used to improve the vision. Also, some people afflicted with presbyopia benefit from surgically implanted lenses or laser correction surgery.

Vision changes in late adulthood

In late adulthood, almost all aspects of vision decline. The peripheral vision becomes smaller, as there is a general decrease in the span of the visual field. The eye becomes less adaptable to variations in light, and many people find it difficult to drive or walk at night as they grow older. Depth perception and color differentiation both diminish with age. Moreover, people are more likely to be afflicted by eye problems like glaucoma, cataracts, and macular degeneration as they age.

Effects of aging on hearing

Around age 30, people begin to experience diminished hearing. In particular, it becomes difficult for people to hear high-pitched sounds. At the age of 50, about a third of all men and a quarter of all women will be unable to understand a whisper. The degradation of hearing ability can be accelerated by prolonged exposure to loud noises, and so people who operate heavy equipment or work near loud machinery are more likely to suffer declines. By the age of 70, about 10% of the population will experience significant hearing loss, and by the age of 84 about 20% will have very poor hearing.

Menopause and perimenopause

Menopause: The point in a woman's life when menstruation ceases entirely. Most women undergo menopause in their 40s or 50s. During menopause, a woman is likely to endure side-effects of reduced estrogen production, like fatigue, hot flashes, and disturbances in sleep. However, some women experience no symptoms of menopause.
Perimenopause: A period of declining intensity and volume in menstruation.
Perimenopause can last a decade, and may be marked by depression, heart palpitations, and headaches.

Theories of aging

Cellular clock theory
This theory, developed by Leonard Hayflick in 1977, asserts that a cell can only divide 75 or 80 times at the most. Moreover, an older person's cells will be able to divide fewer times. This cellular clock places restrictions on the age to which a human being can live, which, for Hayflick, was about 125 years. Since the advancement of the cellular clock theory, scientists have begun to focus on the reasons for cell death. One theory is that cells die because the DNA sequences at the end of each chromosome, also known as telomeres, become shorter

every time the cell divides. Eventually, the telomeres are so short that the cell can no longer reproduce.

Biological theories
There are a few different biological theories for aging. According to the wear-and-tear theory advanced by rheumatologist James Fries, the human body is simply destined to fall apart due to frailty after about 85 years. Another theory, called the error accumulation theory, asserts that human beings die because cells in their bodies accumulate errors when duplicating. According to the free-radical or accumulation-of-metabolic-wastes theory, the body builds up metabolic waste, and especially free radicals, which are damaging and ultimately fatal to the molecules of the body.

Sexual development

Testosterone
Testosterone is a sex hormone produced in both sexes by the adrenal glands, as well as in male testicles and female ovaries. Testosterone is an androgen, and is deeply involved in the changes that take place during puberty. Testosterone stimulates the male body to increase muscle mass, deepen the voice, and produce facial hair. Testosterone also motivates the sex drive and the production of sperm. The diminution of testosterone production is responsible for the slackening of the sex drive later in life. Synthetic testosterone is found in anabolic steroids, dangerous drugs taken improve strength and athletic performance.

Estrogens
The ovaries produce a set of hormones called estrogens, of which the most prominent is estradiol. These hormones stimulate many of the changes in the female body during puberty. For instance, estrogen is responsible for the thickening of the uterine lining, and thus for the initiation of menstruation. Both males and females produce small amounts of estrogen in their fat tissues. Males also produce a small amount of estrogen in their testes. Doctors do not yet understand the function of estrogen in the male body. In middle age, a woman will begin to produce less estrogen, and eventually she will not produce enough to stimulate menstruation. At this point, a woman is said to have reached menopause.

Adolescent sexual attitudes and behaviors

In adolescence, people receive influence on moral issues from a number of different sources. Although parental values are still important, the adolescent also derives much of his feeling about morality from religious sources and teachers. Sometimes, the values of the parents or community are seen as stifling by the adolescent, who then rebels against them. Teenagers are likely to imitate the behavior of their family members, and so youngsters with an older and sexually active sibling, a single parent, or a mother who became sexually active at a young age tend to be more promiscuous. Poor, crowded, crime-ridden, and segregated neighborhoods have higher rates of teenage sexual activity. Most psychologists also feel that the media, and especially television, contribute to a climate of permissiveness.

Adolescent sexual identity

Adolescents are engaged in the turbulent process of developing a sexual identity, a process made necessary and more complicated by the rapid increase in sex hormones. It is imperative for adolescents to manage their behavior appropriately, so as to avoid pregnancy and sexually transmitted diseases. Some adolescents find that their sexual attractions are centered on people of the same sex or members of both sexes. When this is the case, the adolescent is likely to have more trouble establishing sexual identity. Developing a sexual identity is even more problematic for transgendered teenagers.

Sexual orientation

A person's sexual orientation is how he interacts with other people sexually, emotionally, and romantically. The three major sexual orientations are heterosexual, homosexual, and bisexual. Sexual orientation does not necessarily manifest in overt behavior; it may be simply a person's fantasies and thoughts. Nevertheless, sexual orientation is a huge component of self-conception. A number of physiological and environmental factors contribute to sexual orientation. Indeed, the mixture of hormones received by the fetus before birth may have an impact on sexual orientation. The extent to which a person considers or acknowledges his sexual orientation is extremely variable. Some people do not fully acknowledge their sexual orientation until adulthood. For the most part, though, it is believed that sexual orientation is fixed and permanent.

Homosexual and bisexual

Homosexual means having a sexual interest in members of the same sex. A person is considered a homosexual even if they never engage in homosexual actions, so long as they have sexual and romantic thoughts and fantasies about members of the same sex. Male homosexuals are often referred to as gay, while female homosexuals are called lesbians. Bisexual is having sexual and romantic interest in both males and females. Again, a person does not have to act on bisexual desires in order to be classified as a bisexual. More so than heterosexuality or homosexuality, bisexuality is believed to fluctuate over the course of a life.

Transgendered persons and transvestites

Transgendered persons, otherwise known as transsexuals, are people who feel alienated from their anatomical sex. In other words, people whose mental life is distinct from their physical or societal gender. In the past, transgendered persons had only the option of wearing the clothing and assuming the lifestyle of the opposite sex. Now, transgendered persons can receive hormone therapy and surgery to give their bodies the desired characteristics. Men are more likely than women to be transgendered. A transvestite is a person who receives pleasure from dressing in the clothes associated with the opposite sex. This is much more common among men, particularly heterosexuals.

Sexuality in older adults

Because of declining levels of sex hormones, interest in sexual activity tends to decrease in late adulthood. Some adults, in particular men, experience problems with arousal. Also, middle-aged and elderly men and women are less likely to have a regular sexual partner. Health problems and a lack of general mobility can diminish interest in sex. Nevertheless, in 2007 a study of 3000 adults between the ages of 57 and 85 reported that a significant number were sexually active.

Teratogen

A teratogen is a material or action that can adversely affect the development of a fetus. Teratogens can be responsible for miscarriages and birth defects, as well as more minor problems. Maternal disease, advanced age, exposure to hazardous materials, and nicotine are all teratogens. In addition, caffeine, alcohol, blood disorders, unhealthy foods, and a lack of prenatal care all have the potential to be teratogens. Many drugs, both prescription and over-the-counter, are teratogens.

Perceptual Development Throughout the Life Span

Sensory perception of an infant

Recent advances in technology and research methods have given scientists the ability to ascertain the sensory information available to infants. For instance, scientists now know that newborns possess all five senses, though the function of the senses may be primitive. The hearing of an infant is very good, but the vision is poor, because the optic nerve and retina are still in incipient phases. Sense of hearing seems to be operational even in the last two or three months of gestation. Anyone who has seen an infant receive a shot knows that he can feel pain, and other experiments have determined that infants react differently to various tastes and smells.

Development of vision in an infant

When an infant is born, he has an unfinished optic nerve, lens, and ocular muscles. The result is that the vision of a newborn is imperfect. For instance, an infant sees an object 20 feet away about as vividly as an adult sees an object 40 feet away. After six months out of the womb, and infant's vision has improved to the point that he can see a object 20 feet away about as well as an adult sees an object 40 feet away. Eight months after birth, an infant's vision is as good as adult vision. Babies typically develop the ability to focus between two and three months after birth.

Visual Cliff Experiment

In 1960, Eleanor Gibson and Richard Walk developed the Visual Walk Experiments to measure infant depth perception. In order to perform the experiment, a glass surface is placed on top of a patterned material, such that the patterned material is very close to the glass on one end and far away at the other. Perceptually, it appears from above as if the walking surface is on a sharp slope. In the test, it was found that most infants will happily crawl across the "shallow" end, but will not cross the "deep" end, even when coaxed by their mothers. In other words, infants have a natural tendency to avoid what they see as perilous heights.

Development of hearing in infants

It has been determined that the sense of hearing is well-established even during the last two or three months of pregnancy. At this point, a fetus is able to hear music and the mother's voice. In the months after birth, the infant becomes better at noticing differences in the loudness, pitch, and location of sound. Newborns tend to distinguish loud sounds better than soft ones, and high-pitched sounds better than low-pitched sounds. By two years of age, infants can hear low-pitched sounds quite well. Also, by this point the infant will be very good at determining the origin of sounds.

Sense of touch in young children

Newborn children are capable of distinguishing differences in temperature, though they do not seem to mind small variations. Newborns are extremely sensitive to touch, and often respond with reflexive actions. For instance, if an infant is touched on the lip, he will automatically suck. If the child is touched on the side of the head, he will naturally turn in the direction of the touch. This is known as the rooting reflex. The development of the tactile sense helps to develop the sense of sight, as children use their eyes and hands to explore the world. Children often get a great deal of pleasure from handling materials of different texture.

Sense of smell in infancy

Infants are born with a sense of smell. They prefer some odors to others, and react in proportion to the strength of the smell. In particular, research suggests that infants like familiar odors, like that of their mother. Also, infants have been found to prefer pleasing smells, like vanilla, and to dislike smells like garbage. Infants who breast-feed seem to like the smell of the breast milk. An infant will indicate his opinion about a smell by turning his head towards the origin, or by making a face.

Sense of taste in infancy

From birth, people have a sense of taste. An infant indicates his preferences by sucking and making faces. Infants who are given a sweet liquid tend to suck more slowly, almost as if they want to prolong the pleasure of the taste. An infant who is sucking a sweet liquid will appear to smile. An infant given a sour solution, on the other hand, will appear to grimace, and will often refuse to suck. Some babies dislike salty solutions, while others do not seem to care about saltiness one way or the other. A preference for salty foods seems to develop after about four months.

Ecological view of perception

Eleanor and James Gibson developed what is known as the ecological view of perception, which in its most basic iteration states that individuals only have a sensory impression of those items in their surroundings. The objects in a person's environment have what are called affordances, which means that they afford an opportunity for interaction. The degree to which a person interacts with the object depends on his ability. For example, a child will see a hammer as something to bang against the wall, while for an adult a hammer is a tool that can be used to build an elaborate construction.

Visual preference method

The visual preference method, advanced in part by Robert Fantz during the early 1960s, is used to measure infant visual perception. In the basic model, a child is placed in a looking chamber, above which there are two visual displays. A researcher looking through a peephole can determine which display the child is looking at. By placing different images in the displays, researchers can get a sense of the sorts of images that are appealing or innately interesting to infants. Research into the visual preference methods includes keeping records of the length of time an infant looked at each image. This experiment determined that even two-day-old infants can distinguish visual stimuli. Indeed, it was determined that very young infants would rather look at patterns than blocks of solid color.

Habituation and dishabituation

Developmental psychologists use the terms habituation and dishabituation to describe the response of a small child to a repeated visual or auditory stimulus. Habituation is the phenomenon in which repeated exposure to a stimulus garners less and less attention. Even seven hours after birth, many infants display habituation. If the stimulus is altered in some way, the infant will register a more pronounced response. This recovery of the habituated response is called dishabituation. In general, infants have been found to look at familiar stimuli about one-third as often as they look at new ones.

Perceptual constancy

The understanding that physical objects maintain their proportions even when visual perception of them changes is called perceptual constancy. For instance, at three months a child may have some degree of size and shape constancy. Shape constancy is the comprehension that the shape of an object is the same even though it can be viewed from different angles. Size constancy is the understanding that an object does not change in shape even though it can be viewed close-up or from afar. A full grasp of perceptual constancy does not exist until the child is 10 or 11 years old. In particular, infants seem to have a hard time applying shape constancy to objects with irregular shapes.

Intermodal perception

The process of mentally combining information from at least two senses is called intermodal perception. From birth, infants display a primitive form of intermodal perception; they will turn their heads and eyes towards the origins of a sound. As the child grows older, his intermodal perception will improve. Children from 3 ½ months seem to have more interest in a person if they can both see and hear him. This indicates that a child is cognizant of a person as having both visual and auditory components.

Perceptual-motor coupling

In developmental psychology, the relationship between perception and movement is called perceptual-motor coupling. The extent to which a child's movements are based on what he perceives can be measured through experimentation. Over the first few years of life, a child will learn to use his eyes to navigate different surfaces, reach for desired objects, and balance. At the same time, the child's movements will provide him with information about what he perceives. Handling an object teaches a child to draw correlations between vision and size, texture, and weight. Also, a child's ability to move around an object improves his understanding of size and shape constancy.

Perceptual categorization

Scientists have been able to demonstrate that three-month-old infants are able to group similar objects together. This ability is called perceptual categorization, a phrase coined by Jean Mandler, a psychologist at the University of California-San Diego. Perceptual categorization requires the objects to be grouped according to some physical characteristic,

- 32 -

like color or size. This field typically emerges at about seven months of age. As the infant grows, he will develop more complex and differentiated categories. For example, a child at first may only be able to identify basic colors, but with time may be able to identify shades as well.

Perceptual speed in older adults

The speed with which a person can react to perceived stimuli by performing a motor task is called perceptual speed. Of all the cognitive abilities, perceptual speed is the only one that steadily declines with age. This decline is caused by degeneration of the neural impulses throughout the central nervous system. By the time a person reaches late adulthood, perceptual speed can be significantly diminished. This definition is often accompanied by a decrease in working memory. Of course, not all elderly people manifest significant perceptual speed loss.

Cognitive Development Throughout the Lifespan

Attention

Infants
From a very young age, infants are able to focus their attention on particular objects. The parietal lobes of the cerebral cortex are heavily involved in this immature attention span. In the first year of life, a child mainly focuses on objects with a view towards investigating them. Infants are capable of sustaining their attention for up to ten seconds. Infants tend to be more attentive to new stimuli. Over time, small children become habituated to repeated stimuli and pay less attention to them.

Early childhood
In the preschool years, children will become much better at concentrating and prolonging their attention span. First, children will not be able to concentrate, but by the age of four or five, a child should be able to sit for a half hour and attend to a television program. This development in executive and sustained attention is not necessarily mirrored by development in salient attention and planning. This means that children can easily be distracted by more pressing stimuli, and may not be able to concentrate in great detail on the object of their attention.

Joint attention

Joint attention exists when multiple people are attending to the same object and is required to follow a third party, to encourage other people to attend to an object, or to engage in cooperative action. One of the earliest stages of joint attention is when a child's gaze can be directed through pointing, which occurs by about seven or eight months. After about a year, an infant will be able to direct the attention of another person. The development of joint attention is crucial for learning because teaching is based on being able to persuade others to attend to certain objects.

Executive attention, sustained attention, and salient attention

Executive attention is directed thinking related to plans and intentions, as well as to evaluating and correcting mistakes. Executive attention is necessary for monitoring and improving physical and mental tasks. Sustained attention is directed thinking that rests on a certain task, object, or event for a long period of time. Salient attention is the focus on the stimuli that are most relevant to the intended task ability to ignore loud or flashy distractions.

Effects of aging on attention

The process of aging exercises significant influence on attention. Research is centered on three types of attention in older adults: selective, divided, and sustained. Selective attention, the ability to limit the mind to relevant information, declines a little with age. Divided attention, used to perform more than one task at a time, also may diminish slightly, particularly when a person tries to perform more than two difficult tasks. As for sustained attention, or vigilance in attempting a certain task or objects, it seems to decline only slightly in aging adults.

Information-processing theory

According to the information-processing theory, development occurs as a slow expansion in mental capacity. So, instead of acquiring knowledge and skills in distinct increments, a person gradually becomes able to understand and process more complicated and sophisticated information. Child cognition expert Robert Siegler makes no distinction between information processing and thinking. He is one of the proponents of the information-processing theory, which views cognition as the perception, encoding, and representation of information. This model has had a significant effect on education, as researchers have striven to develop the best strategies for teaching students to process information.

Phases

The three phases of information processing are encoding, storage, and retrieval. Encoding is the act of perception, identification, and memory formation. Storage is retention in the memory. Retrieval is bringing back memories accurately and comprehensively. The information-processing model is mechanistic, in that it treats pieces of information as files that are put away, organized, and later retrieved. Proponents of the information-processing model encourage students to develop sound organizational principles for information, just the way a person would clearly label files in a filing cabinet.

Implicit and explicit memory and infantile amnesia

Implicit memory is memory with no conscious components. For instance, people develop an implicit memory of how to read or how to tie a shoe, even though they will never think of any particular instance when they learned this skill. Explicit memory is the memory of experiences, facts, and perceptions that can be recalled specifically. Infantile amnesia is the inability to recall memories from the first two to three years of life. Infantile amnesia is believed to be a result of the immaturity of the pre-frontal lobes, which are essential for the storage of memory.

Development of memory

Before the age of six months, children do not have any real explicit memory. However, between six months and two years of age, the hippocampus, frontal lobes, and remainder of the cerebral cortex grow rapidly. This growth is accompanied by the emergence of explicit memory. Despite this early maturation of the brain structures associated with memory, most people can't remember much before the age of eight. Following that age, an individual is more likely to remember specific events and experiences. There are different theories for the lack of explicit memory early in life: some people think the brain has not quite developed, while others credit the lack of memory on the structure of thoughts or the emotional aspect of certain experiences.

Memory in middle adults

Most psychologists agree that in mid-adulthood people start to experience a decline in verbal memory. However, the results of the Seattle Longitudinal Study suggest that verbal

- 35 -

memory may be at its best when a person is in his 50s. The aging and cognition expert Denise Park believes that middle adults take longer to enter new information into memory, but are able to hang onto it longer once it is encoded. One possible cause of memory trouble is the general overload of information that occurs as a person grows older.

Short-term memory

The brain is capable of retaining memory for short periods and long periods. Short-term memory is very brief retention, often for an interval of only a few seconds. Repeating information helps to store it in short-term memory. Often, a person will retain a short-term memory for just a few seconds, and will never fully encode it in permanent memory. Short-term memories do not become explicit or implicit memories. As people age, they lose their capacity and efficiency in short-term memory.

Long-term memory

Long-term memories are retained for a long interval, maybe even for the rest of the person's life. Repetition helps in the formation of long-term memories, but many of these memories are of singular events. Long-term memories may relate to the performance of certain tasks, like tying a shoe or riding a bicycle. Long-term memory tends to remain solid longer than short-term memory as people age. In particular, people seem to be good at storing long-term memories related to formative and unusual personal experiences.

Memory strategies

There are a number of good strategies for improving memory. In rehearsal, the individual repeats the information to himself or to another person. It can be particularly useful to incorporate movements and gestures into rehearsal, as research suggests that a multisensory exposure improves recall. In the memory strategy of categorization, a person places the new pieces of information in a rhyme or in a group by type. Some people encode memories by associating them with elaborate mental images. A child's memory tends to be better when he explicitly incorporates mnemonic strategies.

Episodic memory

Specific memories of life events are called episodic memories. The remembrance of one's own personal experience is called autobiographical memory. Interestingly, young adults have stronger episodic memory, even though they have fewer experiences to draw on. It is believed that declines in memory associated with aging are particularly significant in episodic memory. Another interesting quality of episodic memory is that people in later life tend to have clearer memories of things that happened in their teens and twenties than they do for any other time in their lives. The degree of recall also seems to be influenced by whether the memory is perceived as positive or influential in the person's life.

Semantic memory

All of the general knowledge a person obtains through education and assimilation into a culture is known as semantic memory. Semantic memories are particular skills, vocabulary, and pieces of information. In order to be classified as semantic knowledge, information needs to be explicable. However, it is not necessary for a person to remember where they obtained a piece of semantic knowledge. Semantic memory remains largely stable as a person ages, though recall may become slower. In older adults, there are much greater rates of decline in episodic memory than semantic memory.

Working memory, source memory, and prospective memory

Working memory is the information held by the brain in order to solve a particular problem. For instance, a person maintains a working memory of progress thus far while completing a math problem. Source memory is the recollection of where a piece of information was obtained. Source memory seems to undergo significant decline as a person ages. When the source of information is crucial or integral to the information itself, it is more likely to be recalled. Prospective memory is the memories concerning things that must be done in the future.

Metamemory

Metamemory is recalled knowledge about memory itself. In other words, meta-memories have to do with memorizing and remembering things. Once a person reaches age five or six, he knows certain things about memory, namely that some things are forgotten, that it is easy to refresh previously learned material, and that simple pieces of information are easier to memorize than complicated pieces. At the same time, a child of this age may not have mastered tricks of memory, like concentrating on the main point of a story rather than the specific language of it. In early childhood, children tend to have a poor idea of their own memories, whereas adolescents are able to assess the extent of their own memories more accurately.

Piaget's cognitive development theory

Substages of sensorimotor stage
In the model of development created by Piaget, the first stage, the sensorimotor stage, has six substages, beginning with birth.
First stage, simple reflexes, the first month of life
Second stage, first habits and primary circular reactions, from the first until the fourth month of life
Third stage, secondary circular reactions, from four months to eight months of age
Fourth stage, coordination of secondary circular reactions, lasts between eight and twelve months of age
Fifth stage, tertiary circular reactions, novelty, and curiosity, between 12 and 18 months
Sixth stage, internalization of schemes, from 18 to 24 months of age

Schemas
Piaget declared that children develop a set of schemas, or structures for thinking, that enable them to interact productively with their environment. In a sense, a child's development is the process of adaptation to his environment. This process includes assimilation and accommodation. Whenever children encounter new information, they must understand that and incorporate it using what they already know: assimilation. This process stretches their schemas, however, and so there is a gradual advancement of knowledge and scope of learning: accommodation.

Cognitive theories of Piaget and Vygotsky

The cognitive theories of Piaget and Vygotsky share some similarities and differences. Piaget largely ignored socio-cultural context, while Vygotsky gave it a great deal of attention. Piaget could be considered a social constructivist, while Piaget is more often described as a cognitive constructivist. Vygotsky, unlike Piaget, did not outline a series of developmental stages. Instead, Vygotsky advanced such notions as the zone of proximal development, tools of culture, and the importance of language and dialogue. Piaget, meanwhile, focused on things like schemas, operations, conservation, and classification. Vygotsky placed more emphasis on language and education, but like Piaget, he believed strongly in the importance of teachers as guides rather than as lecturers.

Bandura's social cognitive theory

The American psychologist Albert Bandura, one of the leading social cognitive theorists, believed that behavior, environment, and cognition are inextricably linked. Bandura and other social cognitive theorists believe that human behavior is learned through perception and imitation. This mimetic quality to learning extends to cognition and emotion as well. In Bandura's model, there are three reciprocal elements: environment, behavior, and person/cognitive. The person/cognitive element is the most independent, and is the area in which the person exercises the most autonomy.

Problem solving in childhood

Children learn different strategies for solving problems as they grow older. At first, children work on recognizing the different characteristics of an object. For example, it may take a child until the age of four to understand completely that objects can be grouped by color, shape, volume, etc. As a child grows older, he will become more adept at rehearsing and organizing information for use in solving problems. The development of the memory is essential for problem-solving, because the child begins to remember similar problems and how they were solved.

Adolescent decision-making

Adolescents are required to make an increasing number of decisions, and their skills for doing so increase rapidly. Beginning in adolescence, people are making decisions that will have ramifications on their entire lives, such as how hard to try in school and who to associate with socially. The adolescent brain demonstrates improvement in abstract thinking, critical analysis, and executive function. However, adolescents are still very susceptible to poor choices caused by emotions and social context and can make poor decisions related to sex, drugs, and risky behavior.

Adult problem solving

In adult life, the ability to solve problems reaches full maturity. An adult should be able to draw on their past and use their fully developed analytical skills to solve problems. Indeed, research suggests that people in their 40s and 50s are better at solving practical problems. Towards the end of late adulthood, however, people demonstrate some decline in their ability to make everyday decisions. In part, this is believed to be due to an inability to keep all of the relevant factors in a decision in mind at the same time.

Theory of mind

Theory of mind is the level of awareness a child has of his own mind and the minds of others. Theory of mind is thinking about thinking; it is the recognition of one's own knowledge, desires, biases, as well as those of other people. Researchers have spent a great deal of time charting the development of theory of mind in children. At two years of age, children are not yet able to understand that another person's mind works much the same as their own. By five years of age, children can understand that other people do not have precisely the same knowledge as they do.

Critical thinking

Critical thinking is a systematic way of approaching a problem. It entails considering all of the relevant aspects of the problem, evaluating possible solutions, and ultimately coming to a decision based on evidence. Critical thinking also entails keeping the mind open to changes that might alter a decision or assumption. In order to think critically, a person needs to be able to keep various facts in mind, analyze data without prejudice, and make connections between disparate pieces of information. Critical thinking is the opposite of superficial thought. Indeed, it is a necessary condition of deep and complex understanding.

Creative thinking

Creative thinking is the unique or unusual approach to a problem. Creativity requires the mind to make uncommon associations, and to view the subject from all conceivable perspectives. Creativity is not the same thing as intelligence, because it is not aimed at coming up with the one right answer to a problem. Instead, creative thinking aims to create multiple possible solutions. A capacity for creative thought is often varies greatly in small children. For instance, some children have a great deal of creativity with language, but are not especially creative in the visual arts.

Scientific thinking in terms of child development

Scientific thinking is slow to develop in children, though many young people show a marked interest in exploring the causes and consequences of things. Unlike scientists, who are trained to remain loyal to a theory only so far as it proves correct, children are apt to hold on to existing beliefs even in the face of contradictory evidence. In other words, children are much more attached to their inherent biases. A child is likely to pervert an experiment so that it will prove what he wishes for it to prove. As children grow, their mistaken beliefs are subjected to so much contrary evidence that they eventually must modify their thinking.

Cognitive development in adolescents

Adolescents undergo an intense process of intellectual development. In particular, adolescents develop the ability to construct imaginative hypotheses and possible solutions to their problems. An adolescent of normal intellectual development is able to think in the abstract and analyze data to derive a conclusion. Developmental psychologists refer to the thinking of which adolescents are capable as either formal operational thought or scientific reasoning. During this phase of life, most people develop the ability to plan for the long term and consider possible scenarios when making a decision. According to Piaget, this is the period of formal operations.

Cognitive development in college students

For most students, the college years are a time of intense cognitive development. Of course, this development manifests in different ways for different students. In the early years of college, students have a tendency to view things as either being all bad or all good. This is referred to as dualistic thinking. As they grow more mature and gain more knowledge in class, students become capable of multiplicity in thinking, which means that they are able to consider several views of the same topic. By the time they graduate from college, students often are thinking in terms of relativism rather than positivism. In other words, students understand that truth can be different for different people and in different situations, and that any truth claims must be supported by evidence and reasoning.

Language Development

Bilingualism

Dimensions of bilingual proficiency
One of the main theoretical principles of bilingual education is that language proficiency for both primary and secondary language consists of at least two dimensions, basic interpersonal communication skills (BICS) and cognitive academic language proficiency (CALP). In order to be successful, students will need to achieve fluency in both of these types of language. Basic interpersonal communication skills are those aspects of language proficiency required for members of a linguistic community to exchange information with one another. Cognitive academic language proficiency, on the other hand, is the set of language skills required to achieve literacy and cognitive development. These language skills are typically learned during formal instruction rather than informal interaction with other speakers.

Interrelation between primary and secondary language
Research suggests that for language minority students to develop of high proficiency in cognitive academic language in the primary language forms the basis for a similar proficiency in the secondary language. Once the student has achieved a high level of cognitive academic language proficiency in the primary language, he or she should be able to make normal academic progress. This is because such a student can receive content information in his or her primary language even when it is impossible to deliver it in the secondary language. The increase in cognitive academic language proficiency in the primary language allows the student to acquire similar skills in the secondary language by increasing the range of comprehensible input. Indeed, research suggests that for language minority students the development of high cognitive academic language proficiency in the primary language directly contributes to a positive adjustment to both minority and majority cultures.

Ingredients for BICS and CALP
There is great evidence to suggest that when students are given enough access to comprehensible input in their secondary language, and are given a positive motivation to learn that language, they tend to rapidly acquire basic interpersonal communication skills. This is one of the reasons why it is so important for teachers to create a positive affective environment for students. When students are encouraged to build social connections with other students who speak the secondary language, they will motivate themselves to develop interpersonal communication skills. Finally, studies have shown that the development of cognitive academic language proficiency necessitates special adaptations in the structure and environment of the classroom, as well as in teaching strategies. A bilingual educator needs to have an additional set of skills to manage the complex needs of his or her students.

English only vs. bilingual instruction
Some people argue that the exclusive use of English in the classroom only provides benefits to students. These advocates of English-only instruction argue that students need to be weaned off of their original language so that they can advance in the classroom. They

suggest that the use of the primary language creates a dependency that can only be broken by English instruction. These people assert that parents should be encouraged to speak only English to their children in the home. Advocates of bilingual education, on the other hand, suggests that the use of the original language is a foundation for learning rather than a form of dependency. They argue that students who have well developed L1 skills are better positioned to succeed in any form of instruction. Furthermore, they argue that the idea of a dependency on the native language is a way of marginalizing other cultures. They believe that students who are told to never use their original language will take this as a slur against their native culture. Advocates of bilingual education think it is important that students be able to express themselves fully at every stage during their academic development, whether this is in L1 or L2.

Advocates of English-only instruction assert that students can learn enough English in one year to just stay afloat in mainstream classrooms. According to these people, even children with low levels of proficiency are capable of understanding normal classroom instruction. To their minds, teachers will only need to make slight adjustments in instructional procedures on account of these limited English proficiency students. For that reason, these people believe that English should be taught as quickly as possible so that students can be placed in mainstream classrooms. Advocates of bilingual education, in contrast, believe that while conversational English can be acquired within three years, the student will need between five and seven years to develop cognitive academic language proficiency. Until students can understand everything that is going on in the mainstream classroom, they will be at a disadvantage. So, students should continue to receive some content-area instruction in L1 until they have entirely mastered cognitive academic language.

Transfer of skills
Advocates of English-only instruction argue that it has never been proven that skills can be transferred from L1 to L2 easily. On the contrary, they argue that in order to obtain maximum value students need to receive instruction in English as soon as possible. They argue that literacy instruction in English is more effective for teaching L2 students, and that students will only hurt themselves by continuing reading instruction in their native language. Bilingual education advocates, on the other hand, believe it has been well established by research that knowledge and skills can be transferred from one language to another. In fact, they believe that this transfer can continue as students receive instruction in L1 and L2. Bilingual advocates believe that language in cognitive abilities have a common underlying proficiency, which if fostered can result in elevated proficiency in both languages. Progress in reading and writing skills in L1 can directly leads to improvements in the same skills in L2.

Models of second language learning

Acquisition-learning hypothesis
One model of second language learning, known as the acquisition-learning hypothesis, posits that there are two separate ways in which an individual develops proficiency in a second language. The first way is called acquisition, and is the subconscious process by which vocabulary and basic rules of grammar are slowly and steadily absorbed. Acquisition is the way that small children learn their native language. The second way in which people learn language is called learning: a conscious study and knowledge of vocabulary and the rules of grammar. In general, this theory emphasizes the superiority of acquisition as a means of acquiring fluency. Although learning can be helpful in speeding the process of

- 42 -

acquisition, it is ultimately long-term exposure to a language that allows the individual to develop an unconscious sense of its rules and idiom.

Input hypothesis

The input hypothesis is another one of Stephen Krashen's models of second language acquisition. According to this model, individuals need to be given information slightly above their ability level in a given language. As the individual acquires the ability to understand the given material, the level should be raised. In order for acquisition to be possible at all, the learner needs to understand the majority of what he or she is hearing. However, the addition of a small amount of incomprehensible information will encourage the listener to continue expanding his or her vocabulary and overall sense of grammatical structures. The input hypothesis can spell trouble for children in bilingual classes, because it is very difficult to set instruction level at the appropriate point for each child. It is for this reason that self-instruction techniques like reciprocal teaching and scaffolding are essential parts of practice as a bilingual teacher.

Monitor hypothesis

The Monitor hypothesis explains how learning grammatical rules affects language acquisition. According to this hypothesis, when an individual learns rules of grammar he or she is able to consciously monitor the discourse he or she hears in the future. Over time, learning these rules of grammar encourages the individual to refine and polish his or her speech. Individuals will use grammatical rules to monitor their speech to a greater or lesser degree depending on temperament. Krashen found that extroverted individuals tend to ignore the rules of grammar and simply plunge ahead, while introverted individuals strive for perfection in their speech. Most language experts agree that the basic rules of grammar will be unconsciously acquired over time regardless of whether they are ever explicitly learned. However, the Monitor hypothesis indicates that it can be helpful to learn these rules as a part of second language training.

Natural order hypothesis

The natural order hypothesis asserts that the acquisition of a second language will follow predictable patterns. For any given language, certain grammatical structures will almost always be acquired before others, regardless of the age of the learner. This supports the idea that bilingual programs should follow a specific order of instruction. There are occasional exceptions to the natural order of language acquisition, but they are so few as to not merit consideration. Interestingly, Krashen felt that the appropriate specific order of instruction will not be exactly the same as the natural order. He felt that in order to achieve the most rapid and comprehensive acquisition of a second language, a rigid sequence of grammatical instruction should be avoided in favor of immersion and interactive performance.

Affective filter hypothesis

According to the affective filter hypothesis, a number of emotional factors contribute to the acquisition of the second language. Specifically, self-confidence, anxiety, and motivation exert a significant influence on the ability to internalize vocabulary and grammatical rules. The presence of significant anxiety or low self-esteem can make it almost impossible for a student to incorporate comprehensible input into the formation of new language. This is known as raising the affective filter. It should be noted that the presence of relaxation and high self-esteem does not in and of itself guarantee success in language acquisition; these qualities merely make it possible for the individual to succeed with hard work and aptitude.

This hypothesis has been used to stress the importance of establishing a positive and welcoming environment in the bilingual classroom.

BICS ⎣6-24mo

In their consideration of second language acquisition, experts distinguish between social and academic discourse. The language skills required in social situations are known as Basic Interpersonal Communication Skills (BICS). These are the basic expressions and linguistic formations that an individual will need to conduct him or herself in normal situations. Students will be using these skills in interactions with their fellow students in the cafeteria, on the playground, and on the school bus. While these interactions are not necessarily to mandating in a cognitive sense, they do require a subtle understanding of context. Most students are able to acquire BICS within six to 24 months of beginning language study. Teachers are often mistaken when they declare that a student has achieved fluency because the student has developed excellent social language skills. Until a student has also acquired a mastery of formal discourse, he or she cannot be said to have achieved total fluency.

CALP 5-7yrs.

The ability to participate in formal and grammatically-correct discourse is known as Cognitive Academic Language Proficiency (CALP). Students with adequate CALP are able to listen, speak, read, and write about content material at their grade level. If students are not considered to have achieved total language proficiency until they can do so. Some recent research indicates that achieving CALP takes between five and seven years. This is because academic language acquisition requires not only learning new vocabulary, but developing academic skills such as comparing, synthesizing, summarizing, and inferring. It is also much less context and academic language than there is in social interaction, so students are constantly forced to utilize their own contextualization skills to understand new information. There is some evidence to suggest that students can use what is known as a common underlying proficiency (CUP) to incorporate ideas and skills learned in their first language.

Theories of language acquisition

Chomsky's theory

According to Noam Chomsky, a linguist at the Massachusetts Institute of Technology, children are born with an innate capacity for learning language. Chomsky called this a language acquisition device (LAD), and asserted that it gives the brain the ability to easily understand word and sentence construction. Brain scans have not indicated a precise location for the language acquisition device, though there is some data to suggest that parts of the brain are ideally tailored for language formation. Chomsky is considered a hereditarian or nativist thinker, because he believes that humans are born with a predisposition towards a language development. According to this theory, all a child needs to learn is the specific ways in which his or her native language utilizes the rules of universal grammar. In other words, the principles of language are innate, and the specific parameters of each language are acquired in the first few years of life. Humans are given a so-called language acquisition device which enables them to acquire the linguistic principles of other languages. This theory remains president and much contemporary thought, although researchers continue to explore the relationship between an innate capacity for language and environmental factors.

Vygotsky's theory

Vygotsky asserted that children do not begin by thinking in linguistic terms. At first, according to Vygotsky, children have mental functions based on their social context. A child will talk to himself while performing a task, in what is called private speech. In Vygotsky's model, private speech is an important step, because it trains the mind to structure activities and tasks in terms of language. Piaget, meanwhile, dismissed private speech as an immature form of expression, merely demonstrating the egocentrism of small children. Subsequent research has indicated that children are more likely to use private speech during the performance of hard tasks, during moments of confusion, or after making an error. Also, the use of private speech seems to correlate with better performance and more attention to instruction.

Learning and interactionist theories

According to the behaviorist B.F. Skinner, language is developed in the same way as any other behavior, as the result of a long series of reinforcements and punishments. Most researchers accept this idea to some extent, though they are likely to emphasize that social interaction also plays an important role. For instance, the relationship between the child and his primary caregiver is seen to be central to the development of language. The psychologist Anthony DeCasper, whose career has centered on auditory perception in prenatal and infant children, believes that the melody of language is inculcated in a child even before birth. This accounts for the fact that children seem to be able to distinguish sounds in their own language better than they can in foreign languages.

Behaviorist

The behaviorist view of language acquisition, developed by B.F. Skinner, asserts that individuals learn language as a direct response to stimuli. Certain words or patterns of language produce certain activities or events in the external world, and then the individual over time develops a mental response to those stimuli. Correct responses to stimuli are reinforced and therefore perpetuated through time. There are a few problems with this theory as it applies to language acquisition. For one thing, the creation of language is a somewhat improvisatory act, and is therefore difficult to see as a response to stimuli in many cases. Also, many scientists feel that the behaviorist interpretation of language acquisition is overly simplistic, and does not take into account the extreme complexity of language. Finally, linguistic response does not always elicit clear and recognizable rewards or punishments, which suggests that it would be difficult for a child to have his or her responses reinforced.

Social interactionist

The social interactionist interpretation of language acquisition emphasizes the relationship of the newborn with his or her caregivers. According to this model, the child will learn to speak in the manner and syntax of those people who speak to him or her. The child's ever expanding knowledge of the world and linguistic context will give him or her tools for understanding language. According to the social interactionists, the child will begin to establish goals in the world and will need to devise linguistic strategy for achieving them. The child will draw upon the linguistic and nonlinguistic utterances that he or she has heard, and will use this information in combination with other knowledge to achieve his or her ends. The social interactionist model is useful, but like the nativist approach it does not

- 45 -

provide an explanation for the startling ability to improvise language exhibited by even very young children.

Cognitive

Piaget: 4 stages cognitive development

The cognitive model of language acquisition, developed by Piaget, asserts that individuals develop linguistic skills in order to control their environments. Piaget outlined four basic stages of cognitive development: <u>sensorimotor intelligence</u> (0 to 2 years), in which the child learns to physically handle the objects of the external world; <u>preoperational thought</u> (2 to 7 years), in which the child improves physically and begins to think conceptually; <u>concrete operations</u> (seven to 11 years), in which the child's develops logical thinking skills; and <u>formal operations</u> (11 to 15 years), in which the child begins to think abstractly and can develop mental hypotheses. As the child moves through these stages, he or she will work through various strategies of language use. In the assimilation phase, the child uses a known word to describe a new object or concept until he or she is corrected. Any accommodation phase, the child learns to correct his or her own errors of linguistic identification. In the equilibrium phase, the child uses the right word to describe the object.

Major language components

Phonology
The way a language sounds is known as its phonological system. The smallest distinguishable unit of sound that can hold meaning in a given language is known as a phoneme. Each human language has a different set of phonemes. Each of these sets is relatively small, compared to the entire set of possible sounds that can be made by the human voice. For instance, many languages do not distinguish between the plosive p or b, as we do in English. Individuals who speak these languages are incapable of telling the word pan from the word ban because they are not used to differentiating the voiced b from the unvoiced p.

Morphology
The morphology of a language is a system by which words are constructed out of letters. The smallest meaningful unit of a morphological system is known as a morpheme. Morphemes may appear by themselves as coherent words, but also may be combined with other morphemes to form more complex words. For instance, the morpheme boy can stand by itself, but it can also be combined with the morpheme –s to form boys. Every language has a distinct morphology, but there may be many exceptions to the basic rules of the system. English in particular is notorious for its morphological exceptions. Students of language should be aware that words are constructed in a systematic way, just as sentences and paragraphs are.

Syntax
The syntax of a language is the basic structure of the sentences. Syntax is distinguished from grammar by the fact that grammar offers recommendations for proper syntax, wherein syntax is the entire collection of proper and improper formulations. Utterances that appear crude and ungrammatical will still be understandable if they are placed into a standard acceptable syntax. Syntax, then, is the basic set of linguistic rules that must be followed in order for linguistic expressions to be understood. Grammar, on the other hand, is the set of rules that must be followed in order to attain a certain, somewhat arbitrary standard of acceptable expression. The concept of a standard of language has been frequently debated in bilingual education.

Phonetics
Phonetics is the study of the sounds made during human speech. These sounds, known in the discipline as "phones," have distinct properties with respect to their production, audition, and perception. Phonetics is distinct from phonology embedded deals with real, measurable sounds, rather than abstract or arbitrary sound units like phonemes. In other words, phonetics focuses on specific sounds and does not concern itself with the context in which these sounds are used. There is no consideration of semantics in the field of phonetics. There are three main areas of research in phonetics. Articulatory phonetics focuses on the precise positions and movements of the speech organs. Acoustic phonetics focuses on the properties of sound waves and their reception by the inner ear. Auditory phonetics focuses on the process by which the brain forms a perceptual representation of phonetic input.

Semantics
The semantics of the language are the meanings of its words. Basic semantics studies explore the denotations and connotations of words. The denotation of a word is the thing or set of things to which it refers. The word table, for instance, denotes a four-legged, flat-topped piece of furniture. Of course, this word may have other denotations, as for instance a chart of data or an underground collection of water. The connotation of a word is the set of judgments and references that accompany a word. For example, the word idealist denotes someone loyal to a particular idea, but it connotes a person out of touch with mundane matters. Every language is a mass of ambiguous denotations and connotations.

Pragmatics
The pragmatics of a language is the system by which it is used in social interactions. The ways in which people use language with one another are determined by the type of expression required as well as the relationship of the speaker with his or her audience. Similar linguistic utterances can have vastly different pragmatic utility depending on their context. For example, the words will you go out with me have a different meaning when they are uttered by a young man to a young woman that when they are uttered by someone wanting to go outside to throw the Frisbee! People that fluently speak a given language will have an intuitive understanding of the pragmatics systems in that language. Indeed, this type of understanding often only comes with long experience.

Language-specific listening in the first year of a child's life

Patricia Kuhl performed a series of experiments about the response of infants to sounds, and concluded that during the first six months of life a child will respond to phonemes drawn from all sorts of different languages. Between six months and a year, however, a child's ability to perceive differences in sounds from the language spoken by his parents improves a great deal. This improvement is accompanied by a diminished ability to recognize distinct sounds in foreign languages.

Sequence of baby language sounds

All babies pass through a similar sequence of vocalizations during their first year. At first they cry, demonstrating three different types. The most common is rhythmic, and is believed to express hunger primarily. There are also special cries to indicate anger and pain. At about two to four months of age, a baby will begin to coo. Cooing is a gurgling sort of sound, typically uttered in pleasure. After about six months, a baby will begin to babble, or issue a series of consonants followed by vowels. The most common consonant sounds made by babies are those associated with the letters b, d, m, n, t, and w.

Receptive vocabulary vs. spoken words

Even before they can speak, infants are able to understand the meanings of some words. For instance, five-month-olds often seem to recognize their own names, and by a year or so children should have a vocabulary of approximately fifty words. The words that a child understands, as distinguished from those he can speak, are called the child's receptive vocabulary. At a year and a half, a child should have a spoken vocabulary of about fifty words. Once the child reaches the age of two, he should have a spoken vocabulary of about 200 words. This rapid growth is known as a vocabulary spurt.

Language milestones during the first 24 months

Children of all nationalities and ethnicities go through the same milestones in language acquisition. From birth, all children cry, and after a few months all children make cooing sounds. After five months, children begin to understand particular words, and by six months most are babbling. After seven or so months of development, children demonstrate special understanding of sounds in their native language, and after about eight months a child will begin to use gestures to communicate. After a year, a child is ready to begin saying his first words. After a year and a half, the child will most likely undergo a vocabulary spurt. In the months leading up to his second birthday, the child is likely to begin uttering simple sentences.

Language development in preschool children

As a child moves from age three to age six, he makes a great deal of linguistic progress. At three, children can pronounce all of the vowels and the majority of the consonant sounds, even some difficult ones like str and mpt. Preschoolers are good at noticing rhymes, and often entertain themselves by interpolating new sounds into familiar words (e.g., by saying, "ball, call, dall."). Children at this age acquire the rules of morphology and begin to use plurals and verb tenses accurately. At age four, children begin to use articles and prepositions, and incorporate alternate syntaxes to differentiate a question from a statement. During this period, the vocabulary increases markedly.

- 48 -

Intelligence Throughout the Life Span

Intelligence

Intelligence is a common word, but it is a nebulous concept in psychology. In Life-Span Development, by John W. Santrock, intelligence is defined as "the ability to solve problems and to adapt and learn from experiences." Another definition offered by the psychologist David Wechsler is "a global capacity to understand the world, think rationally, and cope resourcefully with the challenges of life." According to this model, intelligence is not so much for storage of information as the ability to acquire, synthesize, and productively use information. A final definition is offered by the psychologist Robert Sternberg, who emphasized the application of knowledge in practical ways as the best manifestation of intelligence.

Triarchic theory of intelligence

The psychologist Robert Sternberg developed what is known as the triarchic theory, which distinguishes analytical, creative, and practical intelligence. Analytical intelligence is the capacity for assessing information and making decisions. Creative intelligence is the capacity for coming up with unique solutions and inventing new forms. Practical intelligence is the application of knowledge in real-world situations. People may have different levels of ability in these three forms of intelligence. Many students who have high levels of creative intelligence do not do well in school because they are not as adept in analytical and practical areas.

Gardner's multiple intelligences theory

The psychologist Howard Gardner spent his career working with gifted children, and developed a model of intelligence with nine categories. These categories are logical-mathematical, verbal-linguistic, visual-spatial, bodily-kinesthetic (related to movements and physical orientation), musical, interpersonal, interpersonal (related to self-understanding), naturalist, and existentialist (related to knowledge about fundamental aspects of life). Some critics have wondered whether all of these categories are really forms of intelligence, or whether they are simply aptitudes or skills developed by certain people.

Fluid and crystallized intelligence

Fluid intelligence: The ability to reason abstractly and handle unique and new situations. Fluid intelligence is assessed mainly with nonverbal materials, like puzzles, mazes, and block designs. Fluid intelligence tends to decline in middle adulthood.
Crystallized intelligence: Knowledge and understanding developed through education and life experience. Crystallized intelligence is typically measured with achievement testing. An individual's crystallized intelligence grows with age; it does not begin to diminish until at least the person's 60s or 70s.

Cognitive style

A person's cognitive style is the way he organizes and produces information. Different people find it easier to obtain information in different ways. For instance, some people prefer to have information presented visually, while others have better retention of information that they hear. Still others prefer to learn through direct, hands-on experience. In recent decades, education has begun to focus on tailoring instruction to the cognitive style of the learner. Research suggests that when people are taught in a way aligned with their cognitive style, they learn more and retain what they have learned for longer.

Intelligence tests

Intelligence tests like the Wechsler scales and the Stanford-Binet tests are used to predict academic performance and place children in special education classes. However, it is important not to overemphasize the results of these intelligence tests. In particular, teachers should avoid setting high or low expectations for a child based on test performance, since environmental and maturity issues can cause students to test poorly or well. Also, it should be remembered that many other factors besides IQ contribute to academic success. Extremely diligent students can often make up for poor performance on intelligence assessments. Finally, teachers should remember that all students have some strong areas and some weak areas.

IQ

Intelligence quotient, commonly abbreviated as IQ, is a measure of intellectual capacity. It is calculated by dividing mental age by chronological age and multiplying by 100. Of course, there are a number of ways to derive mental age. If a person has a mental age greater than his chronological age, his IQ will be higher than 100. If the two are equal, the person will have an IQ of 100. Intelligence quotient was first advanced as a concept by William Stern in 1912 who built on the work of the French psychologist Alfred Binet's explorations of mental age.

Stanford-Binet tests

The Stanford-Binet tests are intelligence assessments. They were introduced in 1905 at the request of the French Ministry of Education. Alfred Binet and Theophile Simon were asked to come up with a way to identify children who could not learn in school. They created a test with 30 questions on a number of different topics. Since their inception, these tests have been revised in accordance with advances in the understanding of intelligence and assessment. Many of these provisions have been performed at Stanford University, which is why the tests are now known as the Stanford-Binet battery.

Wechsler scales

The Wechsler scales, developed by the psychologist David Wechsler, are a set of intelligence tests for preschoolers, children, and adults. There are three separate tests: one for children between the ages of 2 1/2 and 7 years, one for children between the ages of 6 and 16, and one for adults over the age of 16. The results of the assessments are an overall score with several composite indexes indicating areas of strength and weakness. Some of these composite indexes are for information-processing speed, working memory, and verbal comprehension.

Culture-fair tests

In recent years, psychologists have sought to create culture-fair tests, or tests that are no more or less difficult for people from different cultures. It is important that intelligence tests assess mental capacity rather than cultural knowledge. One major criticism of standardized tests is that they are more difficult for minority students. There are two types of culture-fair test. In one type, all of the test items are composed of material that should be known to people from all socioeconomic and ethnic groups. The second type of culture-fair test, exemplified by Raven's Progressive Matrices Test, has no verbal questions at all. Psychologists have yet to develop a test that does not favor more educated people.

Influence on intelligence

Most developmental psychologists have beliefs somewhere in between those of the hereditarians and the environmentalists. That is, they believe that intelligence development is based on the combined influence of genetics and social/cultural context. The current consensus is that about 45% of differences in IQ are caused by heredity, 35% are caused by environment, and approximately 20% are the result of the interaction between heredity and environment. These factors are often described as genetic endowment, environmental stimulation, and covariance of heredity and environment.

Genetics
The degree to which intelligence is determined by genetics is disputed by psychologists. So-called hereditarians believe that 60% to 80% of the differences among the general population in IQ score can be attributed to genetics. As evidence, these psychologists cite twin studies in which identical twins separated at birth score much closer to one another on IQ tests than do fraternal twins raised in the same home. Of course, there are many inherited conditions with a clear and proven influence on intelligence.

Environment
According to environmentalist psychologists, the context in which a person develops has more influence than heredity on his intelligence. According to these professionals, mental capacity is learned and developed based on the amount of enrichment a person receives from the immediate cultural and social environment. The psychologist Leon J. Kamin disputes the results of twin studies that seem to prove the importance of heredity, arguing instead that separated twins typically are raised in homes similar to their original home in religion and ethnicity. In other words, separated twins are not raised in especially different environments.

Social Development Throughout the Life Span

Anger and aggression

Boys and girls both feel anger, but they are taught to express it in different ways. For instance, girls exhibit physical aggression much less often than boys do, regardless of age, socioeconomic status, or ethnicity. Boys are much less adept at distinguishing an accident from an intentional wrong, and therefore are often react with aggression unnecessarily. A great deal of research has suggested that children who live in urban environments have more anger than children who live in suburban or rural environments.

Aggressive behavior

Psychologists distinguish three kinds of aggressive behavior: undirected temper tantrums, retaliation, and verbal aggression. Undirected aggression is exhibited by children as young as one year old, though temper tantrums tend to peak around age two and decline gradually afterwards. Retaliation and verbal aggression, on the other hand, increase markedly after age three. During preschool, children seem to show a great deal of progress in regulating aggression. However, some children are less successful at this, and have a much higher probability of demonstrating violent behavior later in life.

Bullying
Bullying is intentional and repeated aggressive behavior toward a weaker party. A bully can act independently or in a group, and may direct his behavior towards one or more people. Bullies often select their victims because of a perceived difference, like ethnicity or religion. The bullying behavior may include teasing, name-calling, sexual harassment, or even violence. Males are much more likely to engage in physical bullying, though females can be equally bullying in their verbal expressions.

Connection to violence in the media
Television has been around for half a century, and research suggests that violence on the screen stimulates aggressive and violent behavior in people of all ages. Unsurprisingly, the correlation between television violence and violent behavior is strongest in those with a predisposition towards aggression. In particular, psychologists worry about the depiction of violence against women, because they believe it propagates negative stereotypes. Also, many people believe that playing violent video games and seeing violence on TV habituates people to real-life aggression.

Causes of rape

One of the main causes of rape is the socialization of men, particularly the extents to which sex is conflated with aggression and to which women are degraded. A typical rapist is consumed by a feeling of power and general anger towards women. Date rape and acquaintance rape are becoming more common, particularly in situations where women are intoxicated. One potential cause of these problems is the male's lack of empathy with the wishes of the female. It should be noted that, although rape victims are predominantly female, there are also male victims, particularly in prison.

Sexual harassment

Sexual harassment is intimidating or threatening behavior that centers on sex. Sexual harassment ranges from off-color jokes and suggestive comments to physical assault. One common location for sexual harassment is the workplace, where sexual favors may be suggested as compensation for promotion or continued employment. Sexual harassment is usually perpetrated by men against women, but it can go the other way as well. Sexual harassment need not be physical or extreme; it can be the mere creation of a hostile environment for women through repeated inappropriate remarks.

Attachment

An attachment is a strong emotional bond between people. Perhaps the most common attachment is between a mother and child. Different psychologists have come up with theories for the formation of infant attachment. For instance, Freud thought the attachment was based on food, though Harry Harlow's experiments in which baby monkeys bonded with a soft but inanimate surrogate mother without food seem to disprove this idea. According to Erikson, care and comfort provision are the most important factors in the formation of infant attachment. John Bowlby, meanwhile, advanced the theory that both baby and mother are predisposed by biology toward attachment. Moreover, Bowlby asserted that typical baby behaviors help solidify the formation of the attachment.

<u>Phases</u>
Developmental psychologists have performed a great deal of research on the progression of attachment. Their conclusions form a rough consensus. According to Bowlby, for instance, there are four phases in attachment: birth to two months, in which any person can elicit a smile or cry from the child; two to seven months, in which the child focuses on his primary caregiver; seven to twenty-four months, in which the child's attention expands to include all regular caregivers; and beyond twenty-four months, in which the child develops the first stirrings of empathy. Another model, derived from research with Scottish infants, has three stages: birth to two months, in which the child is responsive to the entire environment; from the third to the seventh month, in which the child responds to all people; and from seven months on, in which the child show more attachment to certain familiar people.

<u>Adolescence</u>
Although attachment is most often discussed in the context of infancy, people make attachments in all phases of their lives. For instance, even while adolescents are struggling for greater independence and autonomy, they also maintain strong attachments with their parents. Research has suggested that there is a moderate correlation between the attachment of adolescents and parents and the success of adolescents in peer relationships. At the same time, adolescents who have strong attachments with their parents are less likely to become juvenile delinquents or to abuse substances. It seems that adolescents who form strong attachments with their parents are better able to form romantic attachments later in life.

<u>RAD</u>
Reactive attachment disorder, or RAD, is diagnosed in children who have a hard time forming attachments. Such children seem withdrawn and inhibited, do not look to others for comfort, and do not seem to differentiate between caregivers. Children may also receive

- 53 -

this diagnosis if they seek attention from all people, with no special preference for their parents or primary caregivers. There are a number of possible causes of reactive attachment disorder, including neglect during infancy, frequent changes in caregiver, and low emotional affect on the part of caregivers.

Gender schema theory

The gender schema theory asserts that children begin to create gender types as they create gender schema, or cognitive frameworks about the behaviors and characteristics that are considered masculine or feminine in their culture. In the first few years of life, a child learns to organize the world in terms of masculine and feminine concepts, according to signs received from the culture at large. Indeed, many developmental psychologists believe that differences in genitalia are less important for children than differences in perception and treatment in society. Children are consistently receiving cues related to clothing, hygiene, grooming, activities, and jobs, some of which are defined by the culture as masculine, while others are defined as feminine.

Social cognitive theory of gender

The social cognitive theory of gender asserts that awareness of gender norms is created by the observation and imitation of adults and older children. Also, children develop their awareness of gender roles through rewards and punishments. From birth, boys and girls are treated differently by most people. Moreover, boys and girls are discouraged from behaving in ways that are not considered appropriate to their gender. When children act in ways that are considered correct for their gender, they are rewarded. In these ways, children learn how they are meant to behave right from the start.

Gender cleavage

Gender cleavage, commonly referred to as gender segregation, is the tendency of children to align themselves with members of the same gender group. Gender cleavage emerges during the early school years, and continues through adolescence. Although a first grader will probably play with both boys and girls, he is likely to have a best friend from his own gender group. In third grade, gender cleavage is in full effect, though it does not peak until fifth grade. In part, gender cleavage is the result of the socialization of boys and girls in the United States. There are different roles and expectations for boys and girls, so they tend to associate with people who share those characteristics.

Development of gender roles

Through words and actions, parents communicate information about gender roles to their children. For instance, boys are often taught not to cry, with the implication that this is not masculine behavior. Also, parents participate in different activities with their children depending on gender. Boys may be pushed to participate in sports, while girls may be pushed towards participation in dance. Girls are often expected to excel in the arts, while boys are more likely to be pushed towards math and science. Parents even communicate gender information with nicknames. For instance, many of the nicknames given to boys (Rocky or Buster, for example) connote strength. Some research has suggested that there is greater enforcement of gender norms with regard to males than females.

Gender stereotypes

To some extent, our society views certain characteristics as positive when they are exhibited by one gender, and negative when they are exhibited by the other. For instance, strength and independence are often praised in a boy, but criticized in a girl. Nurturing and empathy, on the other hand, are positive female traits that may be criticized when exhibited by a male. These stereotypes are gradually softening, as more women find jobs in politics and business, and more men take on roles as caregivers. Nevertheless, stereotypes are very persistent with regard to gender roles, and children still acquire specific expectations and role characteristics.

Gender differences

Many of the perceived differences between genders are artificial, but there are some real differences between males and females. For instance, females tend to have more body fat than males, and tend to be smaller physically. Females tend to live longer, and have less incidence of physical and mental disorder. The brains of females and males are similar, and indeed there is no research to suggest that one or the other gender is better at math, science, or the arts. It does seem that boys are more physically aggressive, though females can be equally aggressive with their words.

Ethological theory of development

The ethological theory of development, which emphasizes the importance of biology and evolution on behavior, was primarily advanced by the zoologist Konrad Lorenz. He studied the imprinting behavior displayed by newborn gray lag geese. He noticed that these geese follow the first moving object that comes into their field of vision. In other words, these geese were very quick to make a connection with another living creature, regardless of the identity of that creature. This observation was later expanded by John Bowlby, who proposed that children who make a strong early connection to a caregiver tend to develop better interpersonal skills. At the same time, a negative or weak connection between child and caregiver can create problems that last a lifetime.

Peer status

Developmental psychologists have identified five peer or sociometric statuses, indicating the degree to which a child is favored by his peers. These statuses are typically determined by asking children to rate their classmates in popularity. A popular child is frequently named as a best friend, and is disliked by very few classmates. An average child receives both positive and negative reviews. A neglected child is not disliked especially, but is rarely named as a best friend. A rejected child is actively disliked and also rarely named as a best friend. A controversial child is frequently named as a best friend, but is also frequently disliked.

Peer pressure

Peer pressure pushes children to act according to the norms of their peer group. Of course, the norms of the peer group may be quite distinct from the norms of society at large. For instance, adolescents are often subject to peer pressure encouraging them to smoke, shoplift, or be promiscuous. At the same time, some children are subject to peer pressure that encourages them to study hard and follow the rules. Research suggests that children feel the influence of peer pressure the most around the eighth or ninth grade. Indeed, one of the primary tasks of the years between 14 and 18 is to develop the ability to withstand peer pressure and maintain one's own system of morals.

Peer groups

As a person moves from middle childhood into adolescence, his peer group becomes one of the most important factors in his socialization. A peer group can be just a few people, or it can be a large community. The peer group is typically defined by its reputation or its participation in a certain activity. For instance, a peer group could be made up of excellent students, smokers, or soccer players. A smaller group, known as a clique, contains just a few members with very similar popularity level or interests. Membership and sense of belonging to a clique is extremely important for preadolescents, but less so for older teens. By the later teen years, people seem to be less interested in group conformity, and more involved in individual and romantic relationships.

Moral development

Moral development is the process of acquiring the values, conventions, and rules of right and wrong behavior in a culture. Moral development also includes learning how to apply these abstract values to daily conduct. Morals are acquired from parents through both explicit instruction and observation. Also, children learn the morals of their society by observing community leaders, like teachers and religious figures. In large part, children learn about morals by interacting with other people, whether children their own age or adults.

Theories
There are a number of theories about the development of moral behavior. Freud, for instance, suggested that conscience is a natural reaction to guilt. Albert Bandura and Walter Mischel, two cognitive learning psychologists, wrote that moral behavior was learned through a process of social interactions. The developmental psychologists Piaget and Kohlberg asserted that moral development takes place at distinct stages. Piaget's model has two stages, while Kohlberg's has three levels and six stages. In the 1970s, the work of psychologist Carol Gilligan indicated that women develop morality in different ways.

Kohlberg's theory: In Kohlberg's model of moral development, there are three levels, each of which has two stages.
Level one, *pre-conventional morality*, is the determination of good and bad behavior that is contingent on perceived rewards and punishments.
> Stage one, *obedience and punishment orientation*: The child obeys the rules to avoid punishment.
> Stage two, *individualism and exchange*: Children behave well on the premise that it will induce good behavior towards them.
Level two, *conventional morality*:
> Stage three, *mutual intrapersonal expectations, relationships, and interpersonal conformity*: In this stage, children adopt the standards of behavior of their parents.
> Stage four, *social systems morality*: Behavior is based on the social order and social conceptions of justice and duty.

Level three, *post-conventional morality*:
> Stage five, *the social contract or utility and individual rights*: A person begins to focus on essential human rights.
> Stage six, *universal ethical principles*: A person focuses on following his conscience.

Gilligan's theory: According to Carol Gilligan and other feminist psychologists, the work of Freud, Piaget, and Kohlberg mainly applies to men. Gilligan asserted that men and women view morality differently. For example, men are more interested in justice and fairness, while women emphasize compassion and interpersonal communication. According to the research performed by Gilligan and her colleagues, women tend to interpret moral dilemmas with an emphasis on maintaining harmonious relationships. Also, female children are more likely to base their morality on the perceived behavior of other people.

Prosocial behavior

Compassionate or helpful behavior performed without expectation of compensation is called prosocial behavior. The behavior does not have to be especially active: it can be as simple as expressing interest in another person. Prosocial behavior has been observed in young children, who will spontaneously share toys and initiate taking turns on play equipment. Small children will also try to comfort another person, including a parent, who appears sad. As a person gets older, his prosocial behavior typically increases.

Altruism and empathy
Altruism is positive behavior performed with no expectation of reward or personal benefit. Older children tend to demonstrate altruism more often than preschoolers. For most children, the development of altruistic behavior is accompanied by greater ability to imagine the mental lives of other people. This awareness is often called empathy. A person exhibits empathy by vicariously imagining another person's perspective, and by considering this perspective when making decisions. Compassionate and helpful behavior is often the result of empathy.

Influences on development of prosocial behavior
Most psychologists believe that the primary determinant of prosocial behavior is parenting. When parents are affectionate with children, it seems to help the development of altruistic behavior, especially when children see their parents express concern for the environment and living creatures. At the same time, parents should try to avoid making their children feel guilty in order to engender prosocial behavior. Parents are important, but they are not the only influence on children. The child's culture and peer group also contribute to the formation of prosocial behavior.

Empathy

At approximately two years of age, children begin to demonstrate a sense of empathy, or the ability to imagine and simulate the emotions of other people. The development of empathy is evidenced by comforting or soothing behavior directed at people who seem to be in distress. Young children will exhibit an empathic response for real people and for the actors depicted on television or in movies. The development of empathy is considered an important step toward the articulation of personal emotions. Through empathy, children are able to experience vicariously a broader range of emotional responses than they necessarily would experience on their own behalf. The empathic response is a controlled version of emotional demonstration.

Risk

In the study of human development, a risk is any factor that has the potential to negatively affect the progress of an individual's moral, physical, intellectual, or emotional maturation. In general, a risk factor actually creates a negative consequence rather than just the absence of positive change. To be studied, a risk must be identifiable and measurable in some way. Smoking and poor nutrition are two common risk factors: they restrict physical and hence intellectual development. To be identified as a risk factor, a behavior or circumstance must measurably and significantly elevate the likelihood of an adverse effect. When a person is confronted with a risk but overcomes it, he or she is demonstrating resilience.

Resilience

Infants
In developmental psychology, resilience is defined as the ability to surmount events that could cause psychological or physical damage. Poverty, extreme or persistent stress, and erratic caretaking are factors that could harm infants and children. However, some infants seem naturally to respond better to these circumstances. These infants demonstrate an ability to elicit nurturing behavior from whoever is around them. By nature, they are easygoing and affectionate. In other words, resilient infants are able to make the best of any situation. Resilient infants tend to be easily soothed.

Children
According to psychologists, the most resilient children have a positive temperament and are outgoing. Resilient children tend to be good communicators, and they are usually of average to above-average intelligence. Resilient children tend to assume that they can influence their environment through behavior modification. This means that resilient children are less likely to depend on others for help or to blame others for problems. Based on their observation and study of resilient children, psychologists have developed some possible approaches to helping all children deal with psychological stress. In particular, psychologists have learned to emphasize personal agency and autonomy in their work with small children.

Stress-resistant adults

After years of research, health professionals have developed a clear profile of the kind of adult who is able to withstand stress most effectively. These stress-resistant individuals typically try to find an immediate solution to their problems rather than wallow in self-pity. They often have explicit personal goals, which they constantly remind themselves of as they make progress. They rely on organization and conscientious problem solving to achieve these goals. Stress-resistant adults generally do not consume large amounts of caffeine, nicotine, alcohol, or drugs. They regularly engage in some sort of focused relaxation, such as meditation or controlled breathing. They also will tend to seek out and enlist the aid of others.

- 58 -

Positive coping mechanisms

The various ways that adults try to adapt and respond positively to the stresses of life are called positive coping mechanisms   . These are healthy, mature ways of dealing with problems, and they come in four common forms: sublimation, religiosity, humor, and altruism. Sublimation is redirecting any socially unacceptable drives into more appropriate activities. Turning one's anger into art, for instance, is sublimation. Religiosity is the process in which an individual reconciles hardship as being a part of God's will or some divine plan. Humor, of course, is a very common way of dealing with stress. Altruism is the conversion of a negative experience into a positive one. For example, people afflicted with lung cancer who speak publicly about the dangers of smoking can be said to be turning a bad experience for them into a positive experience for the community.

Self-awareness in infants

When a child is born, he or she does not yet understand the boundaries between him or herself, other people, and the outside world. For instance, an infant who spies himself in a mirror would not understand that he is looking at an image of himself. At about one year of age, infants begin to develop a concept of the self. It is at this time that an infant will recognize his or her image in a photograph or in a mirror. As a child gets older, he or she will begin to develop a more sophisticated self-awareness, including the capacity to judge his or her skills relative to those of others. As an example, at about eighteen months, a child will begin to become frustrated when he or she is unable to accomplish a task that he or she sees other people perform. Also, children at this age start to understand appearance stability. That is, they recognize that they will look basically the same over time.

Theory of mind

A theory of mind is an understanding or conception of one's own mental state and the mental states of others. Infants develop a primitive theory of mind at a very young age. For instance, after only a few months, an infant will understand that other people are autonomous agents who have the capacity to fulfill or deny requests. Children also begin to develop a sense of intentionality, meaning that they appreciate the purposefulness and goal orientation of actions. At the same time, infants do not attribute intentionality to inanimate objects. So, whereas the infant who sees his or her mother heating up a bottle understands that she is "doing something," the infant also understands that the table in the living room is not acting with intention.

Deception and self-awareness

As children become self-aware, they start to recognize that knowledge may be asymmetrical. That is, they understand that they know things other people do not and vice versa. One consequence of this concept is the development of deception. At about the age of two, many children will attempt to manipulate other people through deception. In other words, children will begin to lie to get what they want because they have a better understanding of what other people know. Although deception has a bad reputation for older children and adults, its emergence is a positive sign of an evolving self-awareness and a more sophisticated theory of mind. With time, children will also learn the potentially negative consequences of being caught in deception.

Self-concept in preschool-age children

During preschool age (roughly between the ages of three and six years), children develop a very detailed self-concept (identity). A self-concept is a complex set of ideas and beliefs about oneself. In preschool, children tend to overrate their abilities in almost every area. They are often quite optimistic about their chances for success in the future even when they have experienced a failure in the recent past. One reason for this perhaps delusional optimism is that they have not yet developed the ability to rate accurately the performance of other people. Consequently, they have no real basis for comparison between themselves and others. There is a psychological utility to this optimism, however, as it encourages the child to try new things without fear of failure.

Early development of racial identity

In preschool, self-concept begins to be influenced by race and ethnicity. In particular, a child's self-concept is affected by the perception of his or her racial or ethnic group by the other members of society. At approximately three years of age, children begin to identify themselves as belonging to a particular ethnic group. Soon after, they start to understand how racial and ethnic differences are perceived by others. One common phenomenon is racial dissonance, in which a minority child declares a preference for the characteristics or values of the majority group. Interestingly, racial dissonance does not correlate with low self-esteem or with a negative opinion of minority culture. It is probably just the result of the pervasiveness of majority culture.

Looking-glass self

Charles Horton Cooley (1864–1929) was an American sociologist who focused on the development of the self in society. The concept of the looking-glass self was invented by Cooley, who used it to mean the idea of oneself that an individual creates based on the treatment he or she receives from other members of society. This theory emphasizes the social nature of self-development, by suggesting that there is no individual essence that is not influenced by social interaction. For instance, if a person is regularly treated as inferior by his or her society, he or she may begin to believe this to be true. The looking-glass self theory is quite similar to the labeling theory of deviance, in which individuals singled out by a society as deviant often live up to that description.

Development of self-concept in Eastern and Western cultures

Psychological research suggests that Eastern and Western children develop a sharply different concept of the self. In the East (i.e., China, Japan, and Korea), children are likely to develop a sense of themselves as part of a larger culture or social web. Eastern children have a stronger sense of responsibility to other people, and they are more perceptive of the interrelationships among family and community. In the West (i.e., the United States and Europe), children are more individualistic, meaning that they focus on personal characteristics and autonomy. Among Western children, there is a stronger sense of competition and a stronger assumption that each person is responsible for him or herself. Western children are far more likely than Eastern children to fixate on the elements of their personality that differentiate themselves from others.

Psychological self-concept in children

As children grow older, their self-concept becomes based less on physical characteristics and skills and more on personality traits. That is, self-concept moves from a focus on external values to a focus on internal values. This shift typically occurs between the ages of six and nine, as the child's cognitive abilities increase rapidly. At the same time, children develop a much more complex self-concept during these years. For children who attend school, self-concept is divided into home and school categories. The child's home identity often has more to do with emotions, while the school identity is centered on physical comparisons and academic performance.

Social comparison

Around the age of six, children start to compare themselves to their peers. This scale, known in psychology as social comparison, leads to a more accurate self-concept. Social comparison is especially important in areas where there are no objective means of assessment. For instance, there is no scorekeeping system for social interactions, but elementary school-age children will begin to perceive which of their peers are better or worse at managing conflicts and making friends. Children can use social comparison to spur self-analysis or to modify their own behavior. Although children still tend to rate their own performance higher than they perhaps should, the emergence of social comparison drastically improves self-assessment.

Downward social comparison

For the most part, children compare themselves to peers with whom they are similar. However, research suggests that in some cases children will opt to compare themselves with inferiors, perhaps as a means of boosting their own self-esteem. This is particularly true when a child is evaluating himself in an area in which he or she, consciously or not, lacks confidence. A downward social comparison ensures that the child will retain a favorable perspective on his or her own performance. This phenomenon is evident in the relative academic self-esteem of students at good and poor schools: decent students at poor schools rate their performance higher than do decent students at good schools.

Influence of self-image on relationships

One of the most important determinants of how a person forms relationships with others may be how that individual perceives him or herself. If a person feels unlovable, it may be impossible for him or her to seek affection from others. If a person has confidence in him or herself, he or she should be able to develop honest and open relationships with others. Though the phrase is a bit clichéd, it is nevertheless true that a person cannot love another without first loving him or herself. In addition, studies have shown that individuals who have a negative opinion of themselves tend to establish relationships with people who treat them poorly, thus reinforcing their negative self-image.

Social formation of individual values

Every individual has a set of values, criteria by which he or she understands and judges the world. Sometimes individuals claim to have a certain set of values even though they appear to act on another. To clarify values, it is a good idea to consider carefully the consequences of choices and ensure that they are moral and positive. Individual values may be either instrumental or terminal: instrumental values are ways of thinking and acting that a person considers important (e.g., being loyal or loving); terminal values are goals or ideals that a person works toward (e.g., attaining happiness). The values of a person and even of a society often change, so individuals should be keenly aware of the values they are promoting with their choices.

Self-esteem

In developmental psychology, self-esteem is defined as the total set of positive and negative self-evaluations. In contrast to self-awareness or the concept of self, self-esteem is primarily emotional. In the early years of elementary school, children tend to have a unified sense of self-esteem. That is, they have a general opinion of themselves as good or bad, and they apply that opinion to all subjects. As children grow older, however, they begin to differentiate areas of performance and can have a variable sense of self-esteem. One consequence of this differentiation is that children begin to spend more time focusing on areas in which they perceive themselves to succeed and less time on those areas where they perceive themselves to struggle.

For most children, self-esteem gradually improves between the ages of five and eleven. Around age twelve, self-esteem often takes a brief dip perhaps because this is when many students leave elementary school and enter middle school. For each individual, however, the level of self-esteem remains within a relatively small range. Children who have high self-esteem tend to retain it, and children with low self-esteem struggle to improve their self-perception. To an extent, this is a self-perpetuating problem because children with high self-esteem tend to work harder and explore more diverse areas of life, which further feeds their self-esteem. Children with low self-esteem, on the other hand, are less likely to apply themselves and take healthy risks that would boost their self-esteem.

Effects of parenting styles
Psychological research has consistently shown that the authoritative parenting style is best for promoting healthy self-esteem. An authoritative parent is affectionate and supportive but establishes strict guidelines for performance. Moreover, the authoritative parent provides an accurate assessment of the child's behavior. Children with authoritative parents are better at self-assessment. When a parent is excessively strict or indulgent, however, the child loses the ability to correctly perceive his or her own successes and failures. These children may become psychologically disoriented and have lower self-esteem as a result. Sometimes, excessively indulgent parents will give their child an artificially inflated sense of self-esteem, which sets the child up for eventual disappointment.

Race and self-esteem
As one might expect, research suggests that the members of disparaged minority groups tend to have lower self-esteem than the members of the majority group. However, this disparity is greatest before the age of eleven. At about age twelve, children become increasingly identified with their ethnic group, and they learn to base their self-worth on their position within that particular group rather than on their position within the society as a whole. According to social identity theory, the self-esteem of minority children often depends on their perception of prejudice in society. When a child believes that prejudice can be overcome, he or she is likely to have a healthy self-esteem. However, children who

see no way around pervasive discrimination are likely to internalize this devaluation and have a lower self-esteem.

Peck's psychosocial tasks of later adulthood

In his seminal 1960s work *The Road Less Traveled*, psychologist Robert C. Peck advanced the theory that people in late adulthood are confronted with three challenges. First, people at this age may struggle with ego differentiation versus the work-role preoccupation, which relates to how a person sees him or herself after ceasing employment. It can be difficult to create a new sense of self after retirement. The second challenge, body transcendence versus body preoccupation, involves coping with diminished strength and health. The last challenge, ego transcendence versus ego preoccupation, is the conflict between impending death and feelings of immortality. In the last years of a normal life, the person begins to accept the inevitability of death.

Social cognition in the relationships of children

Social cognition is thought about relationships and interactions with other people. As children enter school and develop friendships, they must learn to handle adversarial and cooperative situations. According to Kenneth Dodge, children move through five stages in the development of social cognition. In the first stage, the child decodes social cues. Then, the decoded information must be interpreted. The child then considers possible responses. In the fourth stage, the child chooses a response. The fifth and final stage is to enact the selected response.

Adolescent egocentrism

The psychologist David Elkind accepted Piaget's assertion regarding adolescent egocentrism, though he distinguished two characteristics, namely the personal fable and the imaginary audience. The personal fable is the adolescent's assumption that his problems are original and cannot be understood by other people. Sometimes, this can lead to problems, as the adolescent may become possessed by feelings of invulnerability and take unnecessary risks. The imaginary audience concept refers to the common supposition made by adolescents that other people are as interested in their problems as they are. Because of this perceived attention, the adolescent becomes excessively self-conscious, self-critical, or self-admiring.

Wellness

Health professionals refer to the highest state of health as wellness.
- Wellness has a number of definitions: it may mean enjoying life, or having a defined purpose in life and being able to work towards it, or it may mean deliberately taking the steps necessary to avoid disease and maximize health.
- Wellness is different from health in that it means actively enhancing health, not just maintaining good health.
- Total wellness depends on psychological, physical, and social factors. In the general model for wellness, all of these factors combine to produce the individual's complete level of wellness.

- Part of the reason why health professionals promote the idea of wellness is to show people that all the areas of their lives depend on one another.

Family, Home, and Society Throughout the Life Span

Child abuse and child neglect

Child abuse is physical injury or harm done to a child, while child neglect is the failure to meet the child's physical, emotional, and social needs. In most cases, the perpetrators of child abuse are the child's parents or guardians. Child abuse is often physical, like shaking or hitting. It can also manifest as psychological abuse, like name-calling and excessive yelling. Child abuse can be sexual, as when a child is forced into sex or introduced to pornographic materials.

Spouse abuse

Spouse abuse, otherwise known as domestic abuse, is any behavior aimed at controlling or dominating a marital partner. Violence may be a component of abuse, but it is also possible for a spouse to psychologically and emotionally abuse his partner. A person may become isolated from his family because of spouse abuse, and may therefore lose the ability to find comfort or assistance. In most cases, the victims of spouse abuse are female. Spouse abuse can end in hospitalization or even death, so it must be treated immediately and comprehensively.

Elder abuse

When an older person is treated unkindly or harmed in any way, a psychologist will diagnose elder abuse. In almost all cases, the perpetrator is a caretaker, often the victim's spouse or nurse. Older people may be abused at home, or they may be abused in an institutional setting like a nursing home or hospital. The abuse may be physical, or it may be verbal and emotional. Some of the most common and distasteful elder abuse involves exploitation, in which an elder is persuaded to change his will, to give away valuable property, or to give away power of attorney. Sexual abuse of elders is uncommon, but it does occur.

Leading causes of death

The leading causes of death among infants are related to birth defects and under-development. Infants may die in a miscarriage before birth, may be stillborn, or may die during the birthing process. Among children, most deaths are caused by illness or accidents, in particular drowning, poisoning, and car crashes. The illnesses that most often afflict children are heart disease and cancer. The leading causes of death among adolescents are murder, automobile accidents, and suicide. The leading causes of death among young adults and middle-aged adults are accidents, cancer, and heart disease. Among older adults, chronic disease is the most common cause of death, and it is typically preceded by a prolonged period of disability.

Kubler-Ross's stages of dying

Elisabeth Kubler-Ross in 1969 outlined five stages through which a person passes during the dying process. In the first stage, denial and isolation, the person has not yet accepted the reality of impending death. In the second stage, anger, the person rages against his circumstances and blames God or others. The third stage, bargaining, is marked by attempts to compromise or make a deal to prolong life. During the fourth stage, depression, the person begins to accept the reality of impending death and may become withdrawn. During stage five, acceptance, the person acknowledges the inevitability of his death, and reaches a sort of peace.

Criticisms

The five stages of death outlined by Kubler-Ross have been criticized heavily since being issued in 1969. According to Robert Kastenbaum, Kubler-Ross's model is too general, and does not take account of differences between fatal conditions. For instance, some diseases are extremely painful and long, which can alter the dying process considerably. The dying person's gender, age, and socioeconomic status also have influence on the dying process. Research has shown that some people skip one or more of the five stages, and some people regress back to an earlier stage during the process of dying.

Telling a person he/she is dying

There is a general consensus among psychologists that a dying person should be informed completely. Although it can be difficult to tell a person that he is going to die, this knowledge gives the person a chance to settle affairs and say goodbye to loved ones. It is tragic when a person dies with much work left undone. Also, property disputes can arise when a dying person does not have a chance to settle his estate. Many terminally ill individuals derive some comfort from planning their funeral, burial, or memorial service. Finally, the acknowledgement of impending death makes it possible for a person to receive hospice services.

Brain death

When the electrical activity of the brain ceases, brain death is said to occur. Some specialists assert that brain death may only include the cessation of the electrical activity in the higher parts of the brain, even when the lower brainstem continues to function. So long as the lower brainstem has some electrical activity, a person can still maintain respiration and circulation. However, without electrical activity in the cortex and thalamus, the person will have no real consciousness. Among most doctors, brain death is only said to have occurred when function ceases in both the higher and lower parts of the brain.

Hospice programs

Hospice programs do not try to cure patients, but instead focus on palliative care, which is the reduction of anxiety, depression, and pain. The goal of a hospice program is to allow the patient to die without relinquishing his dignity. For the most part, hospice programs are restricted to care for terminally ill and elderly patients. Hospitals often have affiliated hospice programs. Many hospice services work in the patient's home. Employees of a hospice program may be licensed to distribute pain medication and counseling about nutrition and psychology. Hospice programs often have a religious bent, though many do not. Almost all hospice programs intend to include the family of the dying individual in the decision-making process as much as possible.

Euthanasia

Euthanasia, literally meaning good death, is the intentional ending of life, usually to prevent suffering. One common example of euthanasia occurs on the battlefield, where soldiers whose injuries are deemed to be terminal are killed by their comrades. In the modern world, there are two basic kinds of useless Asia. Active euthanasia is the intentional causing of death. For instance, in some places it is legal for a doctor to help a fatally ill patient commit suicide. In the United States, the only state that allows active euthanasia is Oregon, which in 1994 passed a Death with Dignity Act. Passive euthanasia, meanwhile, is allowing death to occur, for instance by removing a device like a respirator, or withholding potentially life-saving treatment. Passive euthanasia may be performed when a patient is in a permanent coma or has a terminal illness.

Living will

Living wills are created so that people can make their health care wishes known even if they are incapacitated. A living will is composed while the person is still cognizant and competent. It elaborates all of the medications and procedures that the person would like to have administered in the event he falls into a coma or becomes unresponsive. Also, living wills typically have provisions for care if the person develops a terminal or extremely painful illness. The Choice in Dying organization is credited with initiating the living will practice, which in some places is called an advance directive.

Death of spouse statistics

The United States Census Bureau reported in 2006 that 45% of married women and 14% of married men will have endured the death of a spouse by the time they reach the age of 65. By the age of 85, 80% of women and 43% of women will have suffered such a loss. The difference in percentages can be partly attributed to the fact that women live an average of five years longer than men, and also that women are more likely to marry older men than vice versa. Also, men are more likely to remarry after the death of a spouse.

Problems for widows and widowers

After losing his spouse, a person is likely to undergo a bout of loneliness and grief. In addition, many people suffer reduced income after the death of an employed spouse. When children are left behind, the remaining spouse has to shoulder the load of raising them, and perhaps will need to assume the role of both mother and father. When a person loses his spouse, he has a tendency to make bad health decisions, such as eating poorly or avoiding exercise. The bereaved may not sleep enough, and may abuse substances like alcohol and sedatives. Widows and widowers seem to fare better when they have a large social network.

Impact of type of death on grieving process

The extent to which friends and family are bereaved after the death of a loved one has a great deal to do with the manner of death. If a person dies suddenly or unexpectedly, the bereaved are likely to be in shock and then intense grief for a long time. If the person dies after a prolonged illness, the bereaved may feel relief more so than grief. People who are involved in accidents that claim the lives of others are likely to endure symptoms of post-traumatic stress disorder like nightmares, intrusive thoughts, inattention, and anxiety.

Decrease in teen pregnancies

Although the United States still has the highest rate of teenage pregnancy among industrialized nations, there has been a steady decline in recent years. Interestingly, the high rate of teenage pregnancy is not accompanied by above-average rates of promiscuity among teenagers. Most experts believe that the reason for this seeming paradox is that contraceptives and sexual education are less available in the United States than in other countries. Part of the credit for the recent decline in teenage pregnancy is the creation of more programs to offer teenagers education about sexual issues and alternatives to sex.

Sternberg's triangular theory of love

According to the triangular theory of love advanced by Robert J. Sternberg, there are three elements to love: passion, intimacy, and commitment. Passion is sexual and physical attraction. Intimacy is honest, close communion with another person. Commitment is the perceived desire to maintain the relationship despite potential problems. According to Sternberg, consummate love is a relationship that has high levels of all three of these components. There are other sorts of love. For instance, romantic love has passion and intimacy but not commitment. Infatuation only has passion, and fatuous love has only passion and commitment. To like someone involves merely intimacy, and empty love is commitment with neither passion nor intimacy.

Current trends in U.S. marriages

Since 1970, the United States has seen a decline in marriage, both among couples with children and couples without. In 1970, over 70% of American households contained a married couple, while in 2005 just over 50% did. People who do eventually get married are remaining single for longer than ever before, and people who become divorced are remarrying at lower rates. In the first years of the new millennium, the average marriage lasted for only a little more than nine years.

Benefits of a good marriage

There are a number of health and happiness benefits associated with marriage. It seems that happily married people live longer and stay healthier than divorced or unhappily married people. In Japan, it was found that married women live longer. Other studies have found that married women have lower blood pressure, lower average body-mass index, lower cholesterol, and less incidence of depression or anxiety. Married men have lower risk of disease, and married men and women both report lower levels of stress. This reduction in stress seems to have beneficial effects on the function of the immune system.

Gottman's research on marriage

In the early 1970s, John Gottman began his research on married couples. His method entailed interviewing couples while monitoring physiological factors life blood pressure,

- 68 -

circulation, heart rate, and immune system. Gottman followed up on these couples every year, and has to date compiled an index of over seven hundred couples. His seven studies comprise the largest database about married couples in the world. According to Gottman, love is not always an enchanted paradise. On the contrary, couples can make their marriages better and more lasting by making an effort and improving their communication.

Cohabiting

Unmarried people who live together and have a sexual relationship are said to be cohabiting. There is a distinct trend towards cohabitation before marriage in the United States: in 1970 about 11% of couple cohabitated before marriage, and now about 60% do. Indeed, it has almost become expected in some communities for adults to live together before marriage, and many people feel that this system does a better job of predicting the future success of marriage. Many people choose to cohabitate before marriage after a bad divorce. Also, adults may choose to cohabitate rather than marry for financial reasons.

Childbearing trends

The average age of a first-time mother has moved from about 21 in 2001 to 25.2 in 2005. In addition, couples are having fewer children, so there is an increase in the number of families with only one child. Advances in birth control have given people more control over childbearing and family planning. At the same time, there are more institutional child-care opportunities, better parental leave offered by employers, and more male participation in child rearing and housekeeping.

Dimensions of parenting

A series of experiments performed between 1925 and 1975 distinguished three important dimensions of child rearing. To begin with, the relative warmth or hostility of the child/parent relationship is important. Affection and approval signals warmth, while punishment and disapproval signify hostility. The second dimension of parenting is restriction when imparting morality. If parents are lax in discipline, it may lead the child toward transgressive behavior. Finally, the third dimension of parenting is consistency in the application of discipline. It is important for a parent to be consistent without being unfair.

Birth order

In the popular consciousness, firstborn children are often expected to be intelligent, obedient, and self-sufficient. Middle-born children are expected to be friendly, outgoing, and ambitious. The last-born child is expected to be creative, willful, and less obedient. An only child is expected to be selfish and highly autonomous. Of course, these stereotypes are not always true, though researchers have noticed some alignment with them. It is believed that these personality differences may be the result of the way children are treated by the family and the society. In particular, firstborn children are likely to develop differently because they get more attention and responsibility.

Adult siblings

Relationships between adult siblings run the gamut from intimacy to antipathy. For the most part, the relationship that siblings have as adults is similar to the relationship they had during childhood. Specifically, it is rare for children who were not close when they were growing up to become close later in life. Most sibling relationships, however, are very intimate, and remain so throughout life. While it is common for older siblings to act as authorities over younger children, this hierarchy tends to break down as siblings age.

Kinship care

Kinship care is any situation where a child is raised by someone who is close to the child but is not his parents. In most cases, the child is being raised by grandparents, although there are also situations in which an aunt, relative, or family friend raises the child. Kinship care often is required when a parent dies or is incarcerated, when a child is being abused or neglected, or when parents divorce. In the United States, the rate of kinship care has risen steadily since the 1990s.

Grandparenting

The role of a grandparent is largely determined by proximity and family structure. Researchers distinguish three main styles of grandparenting. The fun-seeking style of grandparent is informal with his grandchildren, and is primarily interested in entertaining and indulging the child. The distant grandparent usually lives far away from his grandchildren, and does not have much of a relationship with them. The formal grandparent assumes the traditional role of authority figure and imparter of wisdom with respect to his grandchildren.

Dual-income couples

Couples who both work must cooperate when it comes to budgeting and maintaining the home. If the couple has children, the arrangements can become even more complicated. Couples must decide who will handle the various aspects of child-rearing. In the past, it was assumed that the woman would be the primary caregiver, even if she was working full-time. Now, however, it is much more common for a man to assume an equal share of the childrearing duties. Nevertheless, most women in dual-income households report that they do the majority of the housework and child-rearing.

Working married women

Women who work outside the home have the opportunity to follow their interests and interact with a wide variety of people. Women who work have more financial independence and may feel a stronger sense of contributing to the livelihood of the family. Women who work often have improved self-esteem. The personal benefits of working outside the home seem largely tied to a woman's expectations; if a woman sees herself as an ambitious professional, she will not be satisfied to remain at home. Of course, the demands on the time of a working married woman are extreme.

Children's reaction to divorce

There are five factors that contribute to a child's reaction to divorce. Age is important, because it is related to maturity as well as custody settlements. The relative amicability of the divorce is important as well. Children whose parents remain friendly endure divorce better. Gender and custody are the third factor. In most cases, a child does better when he is in the care of the same-sex parent. The fourth factor, though, is the degree to which the custody arrangement is peaceful and harmonious. The fifth and final factor is income, since the child's standard of living may change dramatically after a divorce.

Stepfamily structure

There are three common types of stepfamily structure.
- Stepmother family: Children are cared for by their father, who subsequently remarries.
- Stepfather family: Children are cared for by their mother, who subsequently remarries.
- Blended family (also known as a complex stepfamily or reconstituted family): A marriage between two people who are already parents. Such a family has both a stepmother and a stepfather, depending on the child, as well as stepsiblings.

Intergenerational relationships

In almost all cultures, family is one of the most important priorities. As a person moves through life, he receives different benefits from his relationships with other members of the family. As a child, a person receives wisdom and guidance from parents, grandparents, aunts, and uncles. Later in life, the person will still be receiving guidance from parents, but will also be taking care of his children. Finally, a person sees his children move out, and must deal with aging and infirm parents. The beliefs and attitudes of a family remain remarkably consistent over time, though each generation provides its own iteration.

Quality child care

The quality and formality of child care ranges widely in the United States. A good-quality child-care center will be safe and will have toys and equipment appropriate to the ages of the children. The caregivers will spend time with each child, and will ensure that the child is having his needs met. The employees of the child-care center should indicate to the children with their words and gestures that the child's desires are being considered. Children should have access to bathrooms if they are old enough, and should have their hygienic needs met by the staff if they are not.

Rites of passage

A ceremony or act that indicates an individual's entry into a new phase of life is called a rite of passage. Many cultures have covert rites of passage, as for instance the vision quest endured by Native American youths on their entry to adulthood. Rites of passage could also include cleansing rituals, training programs, and special clothes. Among the Jewish people, the bar or bat mitzvah marks the transition of young men and women into adulthood. Less formally, acquiring a driver's license, getting a first job, and getting married are all rites of passage that indicate transition from one phase of life to another.

Personality and Emotion

Personality development

Freud's psychosexual stages
Sigmund Freud asserted that human behavior is the result of essential physical drives colliding with societal expectations. In Freud's view, the primitive drives for sex and power motivate behavior, though they are tempered by the restrictions of community. The basic personality is established by age five or six, after progression through the oral, anal, and phallic stages. Freud did not see much chance for the modification of personality over the course of life. Mainly, this is because people cannot be aware of what motivates them, much less change it.

Fixation: According to Sigmund Freud, a fixation is a state in which a person is too much enamored of the particular pleasures in one developmental stage, and therefore will not develop any further. When this is the case, the person is likely to overindulge in certain activities. For instance, if a person becomes fixated on the oral stage, he will probably smoke too much, drink too much, eat poorly, be immature, and lack independence. A person who is fixated in the anal stage is likely to be angry and antiauthoritarian, or, if he veers back the other way, overly concerned with routines and conformity.

Erikson's psychosocial stages
According to Erik Erikson, social context is key when considering personal development. Erikson delineated nine developmental stages, and asserted that each of these stages is accompanied by a particular developmental challenge. In Erikson's terms, these are crises that give the person the potential for major growth. According to Erikson, there are points in a person's life when he must either develop parts of the personality or lose them. If these elements of the personality are lost, there will be a resulting malformation of the rest of the personality. Erikson's model was the first to address the entire span of life, rather than just childhood and adolescence.

Factors of personality

Research studies have identified five major personality factors, known as the Big Five super traits: neuroticism, emotional stability, agreeableness, extroversion, conscientiousness, and openness to experiences. In 2006, a survey of 87 longitudinal studies discovered a significant expansion of conscientiousness and agreeableness during early and middle adulthood, as well as a decline in emotional stability in this period. Early adults and adolescents seem to have more openness to experience, though this trait declines in late adulthood. People seem to undergo the most changes in the Big Five factors of personality during the early adult period.

Emotional development

First two years
When babies are born, they can exhibit the emotions of interest, disgust, and distress. The work of psychologist Carol E. Izard demonstrated that after about six to ten weeks, a child

will exhibit a social smile in response to the interest and smiles of other people. After about three or four months, an infant will develop the emotions of surprise, sadness, and anger. Between five and seven months, fear seems to emerge, and a little later shyness and shame accompany the emergence of self-awareness. In the second year of life, children began to exhibit the emotions of guilt and contempt.

<u>Middle childhood</u>
During middle childhood, people learn to regulate their emotions in ways that are acceptable in their culture. This is in part due to increasing interaction with a broad array of people, like teachers, family members, and classmates. During these interactions, the child learns what is acceptable, and begins to understand how emotional displays are perceived depending on gender. For instance, in the United States it is generally more acceptable for boys to express anger, while it is more acceptable for girls to express sadness. It is very common during middle childhood for girls to express more empathy than boys.

Research of Ruthellen Josselson and Carol Gilligan

In the 1970s, the feminist psychologists Ruthellen Josselson and Carol Gilligan were among those who performed experiments focused on the development of the female identity. This research was in part to the work of Freud and Erikson, which was perceived as overly concerned with men. Both Josselson and Gilligan determined that female identity is created not so much in jobs or politics, but in relationships. According to Gilligan, "Women conceptualize and experience the world in a different voice, and men and women operate with different internal models." The work of Josselson, meanwhile, determined that women assign the most value to issues related to religion and social-emotional issues.

Personality changes in late adulthood

Even in late adulthood, the personality still undergoes subtle changes. For instance, people seem to become increasingly conscientious in late adulthood, and are often more agreeable than they were when they were young. Interestingly, some longitudinal studies have correlated conscientiousness with risk of death. However, this finding has been complicated by other studies that correlated increasing risk of mortality with high levels of neuroticism. The mortality of a person in late adulthood seems to be largely tied to his outlook on life, with optimists generally living longer than pessimists.

Peck's psychosocial tasks of later adulthood

The psychologist Robert C. Peck, in his seminal 1960s work The Road Less Traveled, advanced the theory that people in late adulthood are confronted with three challenges. To begin with, people at this age may struggle with ego differentiation versus the work-role preoccupation, which relates to how a person sees himself after ceasing employment. The second challenge, body transcendence versus body preoccupation, has to do with coping with diminished strength and health. The last challenge, ego transcendence versus ego preoccupation, is the conflict between impending death and feelings of immortality.

Peer relationships for young children

Young children need relationships with their peers so that they can learn about emotional expression. Also, it is in these relationships that children learn how to react to the emotional displays of others. In particular, it seems to be important for children to have a safe environment in which to explore these issues. When children have supportive friendships, they tend to develop prosocial behaviors and become contributive citizens. If children have a great deal of conflict in their early peer relationships, they may become more aggressive and confrontational later in life.

Erikson's stage of generativity

The seventh of Eric Erikson's eight lifespan stages is marked by a conflict between generativity and stagnation. This conflict typically unfolds during the 40s and 50s, as a person begins to focus on his impact on future generations. If the person perceives that he is doing nothing to aid the future, he will stagnate. Generativity may be expressed through parenting, leadership, or teaching, to name a few examples. The important thing is that an adult at this age needs to feel as if he is contributing to the long-term prosperity of his society. This seems to be accompanied by feelings of self-esteem and self-worth.

Levinson's Seasons of a Man's Life

The clinical psychologist Daniel Levinson is best known for the book Seasons of a Man's Life, which is based on extensive interviews with middle-aged men. Levinson's interview subjects were varied, from blue-collar workers to captains of industry. Through these interviews, Levinson charted the general arc of masculine life, and supported his findings with material from the biographical accounts of famous men. His conclusion was that a man passes through many stages between the ages of 17 and 65. During each of these stages, a man must master certain developmental tasks in order to progress.

Learning

Learning

In psychology, learning is defined as experiences or actions that cause essentially permanent changes in behavior. Learning is not just intellectual; it is also emotional and physical. Through learning, a person adapts to changes in the environment, and achieves greater mastery over his actions. There are four basic categories of learning in psychology: instrumental conditioning or operant learning, insight learning, multiple-response learning, and classical conditioning or respondent learning. Learning takes place throughout life, beginning even in the three months before the child is born.

Classical and operant conditioning

The theory of classical conditioning is in large part based on the work of Russian physiologist Ivan Pavlov. According to this theory, the relationship between stimulus and response forms behavior in the future, and can therefore be credited for learning. Pavlov's classic experiment involved ringing a bell for dogs before feeding them. The dogs associated the bell with food, and would begin to drool whenever they heard it. If the behavior causes a response that reinforces that behavior, this is called operant conditioning. Any behavior that can be changed by altering its consequences is called an operant.

Pavlov

The Russian physiologist Ivan Pavlov had his great insight when he realized that his laboratory dogs had associated the ringing of a bell with food. The dogs would begin to drool at the mere ringing of the bell, in what Pavlov called a conditioned reflex. In 1904, Pavlov was awarded the Nobel Prize for medicine. Over the next few decades, he continued his research into classical conditioning, showing, among other things, that a physical reflex can be induced by an artificial replacement stimulus.

Skinner

The American psychologist B.F. Skinner is known as one of the fathers of classical conditioning. During the 1950s and 60s, he performed extensive research on behavior reinforcement, and was able to demonstrate that positive consequences reinforce the behaviors that precede them. From this insight, Skinner created an entire theory of how human behavior could be adjusted and controlled. Skinner's work is particularly evident in modern educational theory, which centers on rewards and punishments.

Sameroff's research into newborn learning

Arnold J. Sameroff conducted extensive research into infant learning. In his 1960s experiments with infant sucking, he noted a difference between suction and expression. In suction, the infant creates a vacuum and draws milk from the nipple; in expression, the child presses the nipple against the top of his mouth, squeezing milk out. Sameroff's research suggested that if only one of these techniques was viable, the infant would use that technique alone. In other words, newborns are capable of making decisions based on positive and negative reinforcement. Indeed, Sameroff was able to go on and show that two-day-old infants were capable of applying targeted levels of pressure to extract milk.

Play as learning

In recent decades, developmental psychologists have come to the conclusion that play is one of the most important contributors to mental, physical, and social development. Also, there is a strong correlation between play and healthy family interactions. While playing, the child learns the boundaries of acceptable behavior, as well as the values and mores of the other participants. Play is a form of socialization. When adults play with children, they teach them the rules of the culture, as well as incidental lessons in language and problem solving.

Gender identification and learning

Gender identification is the process of learning accepted gender norms and aligning one's personality with them. Societies contribute to gender identification by assigning certain colors and types of clothing to males or females. Each society has a set of gender roles and expectations, which are transmitted explicitly and implicitly to children. Some people think that the boundaries of gender roles have weakened in recent decades, but it is certain that they still exist. By the age of three or four, most children in the United States will identify certain actions or objects as feminine or masculine.

ZPD

A zone of proximal development (ZPD) is a set of tasks that a child cannot learn by himself, but which he is capable of acquiring with help from a more advanced person. This concept was advanced by Vygotsky, who identified learning to speak and read as tasks that fall within every child's zone of proximal development at some point. One of the implications of this concept is that social interaction is necessary for development. According to Vygotsky, a child is taught by his social environment and cultural context.

Learning theories

There are three categories of learning theory: behavioral, cognitive, and social learning. Behavioral theories rest on the assumption that behavior can be generated or managed with positive and negative reinforcement. Cognitive theories emphasize the role of information acquisition, organization, and synthesis in managing behavior. Social learning theories emphasize the importance of interaction with other people, in particular role models.

Schooling, Work, and Interventions

Applications of developmental psychology

The influence of developmental psychology is felt in almost every area of public and private life in the United States today. School nutrition programs are based on research into the effects of proper food on intellectual and physical development. Structured preschool programs have become popular in response to research that outlines the benefits of early academic focus. At the same time, schools have taken an increasingly holistic approach in recognition of the developmental psychology research suggesting the necessity of education that targets the whole student: physical, emotional, and intellectual aspects alike. Developmental psychology is behind most of today's standardized testing as well as the curriculum used in both public and private schools. To the extent that parents and teachers emphasize creating a strong foundation in the early years of childhood, it is because of the increasing relevance of developmental psychology principles.

Role

A role is a person's particular niche within a society. Every role has a set of expectations and norms that define how the person holding it should behave. For example, in the case of the role of the father, most societies expect that a person will provide economic and material support for the rest of his family. It is quite possible to hold multiple roles at the same time, and indeed to acquire and cast off roles as one moves through life. Culturally acknowledged roles help to provide a society with its basic structure. Much of the trouble resulting from an individual's passage from one culture to another comes from the difficulty in discovering and occupying an accepted role in the new society.

Role set
The role set is the full group of roles associated with any particular status. A college professor, for instance, must by turns be a mentor, expert, friend, and colleague.

Role strain
Role strain is the difficulty an individual may have in meeting the social obligations of a role. Most sociologists would say that every individual experiences role strain to some degree, as no person is perfectly suited to any role.

Role exit
Role exit is the process of leaving a role that formerly had been integral to the individual's personality. Everyone exits roles throughout their life, for example leaving behind the role of son when one's parents die, or leaving the role of student when one graduates.

Role taking

Role-taking is the process whereby an individual imagines him or herself in the role of another, and tries then to understand the meaning of what the other is expressing.

Role performance

Role performance is the way people holding a particular role actually behave, as opposed to the way they are expected to behave as holders of that role.

Impression management
Impression management is one's conscious manipulation of one's role performance. Successful role management requires that an individual has an accurate understanding of his or her role, as well as the expectations society has for him or her.

Studied nonobservance
Studied nonobservance is the sociological term for when members of a society ignore lapses in one another's role performance, in the interest of preserving harmony within the society.

Home and work roles

It is important that an individual is able to balance his or her work and home roles because it is becoming more and more common for individuals to have to act as both caregiver and provider for the family. The ever more common presence of dual roles in society can be extremely difficult for an individual to balance, as there may be instances where work-related responsibilities and family-related responsibilities conflict with one another. Family and consumer sciences education attempts to teach individuals how to avoid and how to handle these conflicts through the use of successful life management tactics such as time and resources management, problem-solving and decision-making techniques, effective communication techniques, etc. Family and consumer sciences education also attempts to give individuals a basic understanding of what responsibilities and qualities are necessary for the successful completion of each role so that individuals can set better priorities and find better ways to plan their lives.

IDEA

Responding to an education system that failed to serve disabled children adequately, the United States Congress passed the Education for All Handicapped Children Act, Public Law 94–142, in 1975. This act mandated free and appropriate public education for disabled students. In 1990, this act was updated as the Individuals with Disabilities Education Act, or IDEA. The act was amended in 1997 and reauthorized in 2004, at which point it became known as the Individuals with Disabilities Education Improvement Act. This act mandates that children be evaluated to determine whether they are eligible for special education. Also, IDEA requires schools to provide individualized education plans and the least restrictive educational environment.

IEP

Schools are required to compose an individualized education plan (IEP) for all public school students with disabilities. An IEP is a written statement describing the specific educational program appropriate for the student, based on his unique needs. The IEP should be composed by the student, his parents, an independent child advocate, teachers, and the school psychologist, in collaboration. It is considered a legal document that binds the school system to providing the outlined plan.

Learning styles

Visual learners
Visual learners learn through seeing. These learners need to see the teacher's body language and facial expression to fully understand the content of a lesson. They tend to prefer sitting at the front of the classroom to avoid visual obstructions (e.g. people's heads). They may think in pictures and learn best from visual displays including: diagrams, illustrated text books, overhead transparencies, videos, flipcharts and hand-outs. During a lecture or classroom discussion, visual learners often prefer to take detailed notes to absorb the information.

Auditory learners
Auditory learners learn through listening. They learn best through verbal lectures, discussions, talking things through and listening to what others have to say. Auditory learners interpret the underlying meanings of speech through listening to tone of voice, pitch, speed and other nuances. Written information may have little meaning until it is heard. These learners often benefit from reading text aloud and using a tape recorder.

Tactile/kinesthetic learners
Tactile/kinesthetic learners learn through moving, doing, and touching. Tactile/Kinesthetic persons learn best through a hands-on approach, actively exploring the physical world around them. They may find it hard to sit still for long periods and may become distracted by their need for activity and exploration.

Career clusters

One of the main uses of the system of career clusters as devised by the United States government is to provide vocational educators with a simplified way to look at the skills and standards for various types of jobs. The government has developed extensive paperwork regarding each of the sixteen skill sets, complete with specific training required and skills that must be acquired. Oftentimes, vocational teachers will administer a questionnaire to students that determines which career clusters best suit their interests and aptitudes. Then, with the help of the available literature, the teacher can work with the student to develop a plan for attaining the skills necessary for employment in their chosen field.

In this extremely specialized modern economy, it is useful to consider various "clusters" of careers that have similar attributes. The United States government has established sixteen career clusters: agriculture and natural resources, arts/audio/video technology and communications, architecture and construction, business and administration, education and training, finance, government and public administration, health science, hospitality and tourism, human services, information technology services, law and public safety, manufacturing, retail/wholesale sales and services, scientific research and engineering, and transportation distribution and logistics. These clusters have been created in part to aid vocational educators, who may be overwhelmed by the variety of potential careers and can benefit from a system of summary.

Specialization

Specialization means dividing a particular job up into its various components, an allowing one worker to specialize in each. Although this idea has been around for centuries, it has been taken to another level by factory managers. Industrial engineers in the modern era may divide the manufacture of a product by process, workers, geographical location, or chronology. They may plan to develop certain parts of their operation in places where it is most cost-effective, or in the places where the workers are already skilled in the appropriate ways. They must also have plans in place for any errors or insufficiencies that may occur. The United States, because of its diverse geography, offers great opportunities for specialization.

Vocational education

Vocational education is the training of individuals to perform certain jobs. Often, large communities will have separate schools whose sole purpose is to cultivate workplace skills. These schools may work in conjunction with local industries to tailor the students' education to the anticipated job market. Vocational classes and schools may also offer cooperative training opportunities, in which students gain first-hand experience in their field of interest. As industrial work becomes more and more specialized, companies are requiring extensive vocational training and on-the-job experience for their employees. Public vocational education is designed to enhance the entire life of the worker; to this end, non-vocational classes are required so that students can earn a secondary degree as they gain work skills and experience.

Acts and amendments
The Vocational Education Act of 1963, also called the Carl D. Perkins Act of 1963, broadened the government's conception of vocational education. It established some procedures to provide part-time employment to students, and established a federal advisory council on vocational education. It also set aside some federal money for the construction of local vocational schools. This act also established some work-study programs enabling students to get real-life experience while earning some school credit. Some amendments were made to this act in 1968, including some direct support for cooperative education and a renewed emphasis on postsecondary education. The amendments also included new provisions for funding an expanded vocational curriculum.

The Carl D. Perkins Act of 1984 was issued in the hopes of improving the basic skills of the labor force and preparing students for the job market by enhancing vocational education. Specifically, the Perkins Act sought to establish equal opportunities for adults in vocational education, and to aid in the introduction of new technologies in vocational instruction. In order to meet its objectives, the Perkins Act set aside money for research into vocational education, as well as money to ensure access to vocational studies for people with disabilities, adults in need of retraining, single parents, and ex-convicts. This act was enhanced in 1990 with the issuing of the Perkins Vocational and Applied Technology Act. This act sought to integrate academic and vocational studies, as well as to fund better technology in vocational classrooms and better cooperation between the business and education communities.

Cooperative education work-experience program

Cooperative education is a method of providing students with academic instruction and practical, hands-on experience at the same time. As the job market has become more competitive, employers have increasingly valued on-the-job experience, so cooperative education gives students the chance to earn valuable training while not sacrificing their education in other areas. Research has shown that cooperative education increases motivation and clarifies career choices for students. For employers, cooperative education helps create a trained workforce and gives business some control over school curricula. However, observers have noted that cooperative education programs are still stigmatized as "non-academic" by some, and may isolate students from the academic community at large.

Job-shadowing

Job-shadowing is one of the many ways that students can gain some experience in the workplace. In job-shadowing, a student simply follows along with a worker in the field in which they are interested as that worker goes through a normal day. Through shadowing a real worker, students can learn first-hand what skills they will need to hold a certain job and what exactly a job entails. Sometimes, students may discover that they are not as interested in a particular job as they originally thought. For instance, a research study showed that students that originally were interested in fire fighting often changed their minds once they realized the real, day-to-day life it would involve. One of the limitations of job-shadowing is that students only observe; they do not actually practice any job skills.

Preschool care

Prevalence in the United States
In the United States, approximately 75 percent of children receive some care outside of the home between the ages of three and six. When this care is aimed at improving intellectual, physical, and social skills, it can be defined as preschool. The rate of participation in preschool has risen dramatically over the past few decades in large part because of an increase in the number of working mothers. According to the most recent figures, more than half of women with children under the age of six have jobs, and the majority of these jobs require full-time hours. On a positive note, preschool has been shown to improve the social and intellectual skills of small children. This is particularly true for those children who are enrolled in organized and constructive preschools.

Advantages
A great deal of research has been done regarding the cognitive and social benefits of preschool, with differing results. Some studies have indicated that preschoolers demonstrate a stronger memory and greater verbal fluency upon entering elementary school. In particular, research has shown that children from disadvantaged backgrounds obtain greater benefits from participation in preschool. Much seems to depend on the quality of the preschool program. Children who attend high-quality preschools are more confident and autonomous. However, some studies suggest that children who attend mediocre preschools are more competitive and less polite. It seems that participation in preschool is much like parenting: it may be beneficial or damaging, depending on its character.

<u>Characteristics of quality preschools</u>
There are a number of different approaches to preschool instruction, but high-quality preschools seem to have a few characteristics in common. To begin with, quality preschools are led by educated and well-trained teachers. Also, quality preschools have a relatively low ratio of care providers to children. This is especially true for very young children; experts recommend that there be no more than five three-year-olds for each adult in the preschool. For four- and five-year-olds, the ratio of care providers to children may be slightly higher. It is also very important for a preschool to have a defined and well-organized curriculum. Some studies suggest that the content of the curriculum is actually less important than its mere presence because preschool-age children derive benefits simply from adhering to a routine.

Head Start program

Since the 1960s, many school districts in the United States have offered Head Start programs, which provide children from low-income families with preschool instruction. Head Start programs focus on academic content and require a great deal of parental participation. The results of these programs have been mixed. Participants are markedly better prepared for elementary school, but they do not display any long-term increases in IQ or academic performance. Nevertheless, the high school graduation rate for children who participate in Head Start programs is significantly higher than for children from similar backgrounds who do not. Some critics argue that children who attend Head Start programs have other advantages, like committed parents, that are the real reasons for their elevated performance.

Types of day care centers

Day care centers, which may also be called childcare centers, provide guidance and supervision for children outside of the home. Typically, children go to day care centers because their parents work. In recent decades, day care centers have increased their emphasis on developing children's physical and intellectual skills. Nevertheless, research suggests that the primary benefit of attendance at a day care center is social. Some day care centers are run in private homes, while others are operated by religious institutions, community centers, schools, or government agencies. Most states require day care centers to obtain licenses if they serve a certain number of children. As part of the licensure process, the day care center may be required to employ only trained teachers.

Family involvement in caregiving

In most families, one of the grown children of an elderly individual will assume a caregiving role. Often, this role entails bringing the parent into the son or daughter's home, arranging for alternative housing, or establishing care for the parent in the parent's own home. This situation has become increasingly common as the average life expectancy has risen over the past few decades. Caring for an aging parent is extremely hard work, so those family members most actively involved should avail themselves of all community resources and be sure to follow the advice of health professionals. One of the most important things a family can do as some of its members age is honestly and openly confront the challenge, acknowledging the help that will be needed and making plans to arrange the appropriate care.

Community resources for the elderly

Most communities have established resources for aging individuals. There are often senior citizen centers or adult day care centers where elderly individuals can enjoy prepared meals and meet both with health professionals and with people their own age. Many cities and towns provide visiting nurses and homemakers to ensure that the elderly are being given enough care and that their homes do not fall into disrepair. In addition, communities often have a service that delivers inexpensive or free meals to the elderly. Some communities offer inexpensive legal aid to aging individuals who need it, and others have hospitals where the elderly can go during the day to receive physical therapy and free medical advice.

Problems nursing home care

The nurses, therapists, physicians, and pharmacists employed by nursing homes must all meet minimum standards of competence and experience. Nevertheless, in too many nursing homes, medication is used to sedate patients rather than to treat their illnesses. Patients may be medicated to the point that they find it hard to exercise autonomy. When this occurs, the overall health of patients may suffer. If patients are given appropriate care and allowed to maintain some degree of control over their lives, they tend to remain in good health for longer. It is better if patients do not become too dependent on nursing home staff.

Elder abuse

When an older person is treated unkindly or harmed in any way, a psychologist will diagnose elder abuse. In almost all cases, the perpetrator is a caretaker, often the victim's spouse or nurse. Older people may be abused at home, or they may be abused in an institutional setting like a nursing home or hospital. The abuse may be physical, or it may be verbal and emotional. Some of the most common elder abuse involves exploitation in which an elder is persuaded to change his or her will, to give away valuable property, or to reassign his or her power of attorney. Sexual abuse of elders is uncommon, but it does occur.

Home care for the terminally ill

Rather than live out their final days in a hospital, terminally ill people may choose to stay at home. This course of action is especially common when extensive medical treatment is unnecessary. Although the dying person may be comforted by the familiarity of home, there are some disadvantages to home care for the terminally ill. For one thing, it shifts a large amount of the burden for care provision to family members who are likely to be emotionally stressed already. It can also be more expensive than hospital care. Home care is only appropriate when it can be managed effectively and when the necessary medical staff is available.

Hospice care

When hospital care is not desired and home care is not feasible, people may choose to die in hospice care. A hospice institution is committed to providing comfort and care to terminally ill people. Rather than attempting to prolong life, hospice centers try to alleviate suffering. In general, those who receive hospice care seem to be satisfied with the experience.

Moreover, the family members of the ill are often relieved by the arrangement because they do not have to provide medical care or stay on call 24 hours a day. Many people feel that hospice care facilities provide a more comforting and human experience for the terminally ill than hospitals do.

Retirement

American workers spend 10 to 15 % of their lives retired. However, this percentage is decreasing as people work beyond the former retirement age of 60. Many people elect to take on another career after retirement, and many companies offer employees the option of slowly decreasing their hours after reaching their mid-60s. In part, this trend away from retirement is due to increasing cost of living. However, most people pursue a postretirement occupation that is significantly less lucrative, and indeed many people volunteer after retiring.

Atypical Development

Mental disorder and mental illness

The American Psychiatric Association (APA) defines mental disorder as any behavioral or psychological syndrome that increases the individual's risk of injury or loss of freedom, creates distress for the individual, or impairs some other area of functioning. In other words, a mental disorder is a condition that works against the individual's chances of having a productive, pleasant life. Mental illness is more severe and is defined by the APA as a mental, behavioral, or emotional disorder that can be diagnosed by a doctor and that interferes with one or more of the individual's daily life activities. These activities may include things as simple as dressing, eating, or working.

Phobias

The most common kind of anxiety disorder is a phobia, an irrational and intense fear of some object or situation. About one in ten adults will develop some kind of intense phobia at some point in his or her life. Although many prescription medications have been used to treat phobias, none seem to be very effective unless they are taken along with behavior therapy, in which the individual is subjected to gradually increasing levels of the feared object or situation. Medical hypnosis therapy has also proved effective in combating phobias. An individual may have developed a phobia if he or she recognizes that the fear is excessive or irrational, and is unable to function because of fear.

GAD

Generalized anxiety disorder (GAD) is persistent anxiety and occasional panic attacks without real cause. A person suffering from GAD is almost constantly immobilized by anxiety, without a specific reason. This condition affects women more often than men and tends to emerge between the ages of twenty and thirty-nine. People with GAD retreat from life, and they stunt their own development by limiting their interactions with other people and the outside world. There is no one cause of GAD, though some experts believe it is inherited or related to a past trauma. Cognitive therapy, medication, and even exercise have documented success in the treatment of GAD. This can be a difficult disorder to diagnose, however, as the anxiety is not related to a discernible cause.

Panic attacks and panic disorder

Panic attacks are massive feelings of anxiety, often accompanied by hyperventilation, racing pulse, and dizziness. The victim of a panic attack may become numb in some of their extremities, and will usually feel a string sense of impending doom. Most of these attacks climax after about ten minutes. If an individual has frequent panic attacks, he or she may be said to have panic disorder. About one-third of all individuals will experience a panic attack before the age of 35. There are two common treatments for panic disorder: cognitive-behavioral therapy, in which the individual learns specific strategies for dealing with a panic attack; and anti-anxiety medication, which only seems to work well when it is combined with behavioral therapy.

Obsessive-compulsive disorder

One extreme kind of anxiety disorder is obsessive-compulsive disorder, in which the individual is plagued by a recurring thought that they cannot escape, and may display repetitive, rigidly formalized behavior. Individuals who suffer from OCD are most often plagued by thoughts of violence, contamination (for instance, being concerned that they are infected), or doubt. The most common compulsions among individuals with OCD are hand washing, cleaning, counting, or checking locks. Individuals suffering from OCD probably recognize that their behavior is irrational but feel powerless to stop it. OCD will eventually get in the way of the person's functioning in other areas of life, and will require treatment. Though OCD is thought to have biological origins, it can be treated with a combination of medication and behavioral therapy.

ADHD

Attention deficit hyperactivity disorder (ADHD) has a number of common symptoms, like impulsiveness, inattentiveness, and excessive activity. This disorder is diagnosed in many children these days, typically in one of three varieties. If a child is easily bored and cannot stay on task, he may have ADHD with predominantly inattention. If the child acts without considering the consequences and is generally impatient, he may have ADHD with predominantly hyperactivity/impulsivity. It is also possible to have ADHD with both hyperactivity/impulsivity and inattention. Although attention deficit hyperactivity disorder may persist into adulthood, it does not rule out success in personal and professional life. However, people with this disorder are more likely to abuse substances and engage in antisocial behavior.

Suspected causes
The precise causes of attention deficit hyperactivity disorder are not known, though many researchers believe that it is an inherited condition. There is also the possibility that the condition is caused by problems during gestation, like exposure to alcohol or tobacco smoke. Children with ADHD seem to have below-average birth weight. Other researchers have proposed that food additives, allergies, excessive television watching, and bad parenting are to blame for the increase in attention deficit hyperactivity disorder. Brain scans indicate that children with ADHD do not develop full thickness of the cerebral cortex until three years after other children.

Treatment
Doctors and psychologists usually treat attention deficit hyperactivity disorder with a combination of education and behavior management. Therapy by itself does not seem to solve the problem. Perhaps one of the best solutions for children with this condition is regular and vigorous exercise. The two drugs most often used to treat ADHD are Ritalin and Adderall, stimulants that seem to focus the attention. However, there is a growing wave of criticism against administrating psychoactive drugs to children with ADHD. In particular, many critics charge that these drugs are overprescribed and often prescribed to the wrong children.

Autism

There are a range of pervasive developmental disorders that fall under the rubric of autism. These conditions typically manifest as repetitive behavior and trouble with communication and social interaction. Autism may be mild or severe. If it is severe, it typically appears during the first three years of life, when a child communicates poorly or performs strange behaviors repeatedly. Asperger's syndrome is a mild form of autism, in which the child communicates well but has a difficult time with nonverbal communication. Children with Asperger's syndrome are likely to develop narrow, intense interests.

Causes

At present, researchers do not understand the causes of autism. It is not believed that parenting can cause autism, and most authorities do not define autism as a mental illness. However, there is some correlation between autism and intellectual disabilities. In some cases, genetics seem to contribute to autism. For instance, congenital rubella syndrome, untreated PKU, fragile X syndrome, tuberous sclerosis, and fetal alcohol syndrome all correlate with autism. Vaccines containing thimerosal are blamed by some for a recent increase in autism, but this has yet to be proven by scientific testing. Brain scans have demonstrated slight abnormalities in brain structure and neurotransmitter function in the autistic brain. Also, some studies have identified a link between autism and too many or too few pieces on the DNA of chromosome 16.

Treatments or interventions

Autism cannot be cured, but autistic people can be taught to live healthy, fulfilling lives. As with many learning disabilities, autism is treated best if it is diagnosed early. Most autistic children require individual instruction and a high degree of order. Autistic children tend to thrive in routinized environments. It may be necessary to use behavior modification or behavioral interventions to reduce the frequency of damaging repetitive behaviors. Positive reinforcement works in some cases. Autism is not treated with medication, though related symptoms like hyperactivity or epilepsy may be managed pharmaceutically.

Asperger's Syndrome

Asperger's Syndrome refers to a subset of children on the autism spectrum scale. This disorder affects mostly males. These children have deficits in social interactions.

Their repetitive behaviors are similar to other children with autism; however, their language and intellectual abilities are at the higher end of the spectrum scale. Given social interaction problems, language issues are primarily due to poor pragmatics. Therefore improving the social context of language is the training goal when working with these children. Given the propensity to engage in repetitive behaviors, these children must learn to reduce or eliminate perseverant language.

Challenges faced by disabled people

In the United States, disability is generally defined as any condition that restricts a major life activity. Disabilities may be physical or mental. There are about 50 million people with some form of disability in the United States. Despite the passage of the Americans with Disabilities Act in 1990, there are still many physical restrictions for the disabled. In particular, older buildings may not be outfitted with proper modifications for the disabled.

More generally, social discrimination against the disabled is quite prevalent. Many disabled people complain that their disability becomes the focal point of their relations with other people and that they are unable to discuss anything else. People with disabilities may suffer from chronic low self-esteem, not because of their own limitations but because of how they are treated by others.

Emotional development issues related to physical disability

Children with a physical disability may have abnormal or slower emotional development in part because these children may not be capable of making the normal physical responses to stimuli. Often, a child with a physical disability has a typical emotional response, but he or she expresses it in such a way as to be misunderstood by his or her caregivers. As a result, the caregiver alters his or her approach, and the child's emotional development is affected. This is especially true in the relationship between a mother and her child. Mothers must learn the differences in response related to certain disabilities so that they can be careful to avoid interpreting disability as rejection. Too often, disabled children receive less care from their parents, not because of a lack of love but because of a misinterpretation of the disabled child's behavior and mood.

Physical disability and cognitive and social development

In the first years of life, a considerable amount of learning occurs during physical interaction with the immediate environment. For disabled children, problems with motor skills and self-control can make interaction difficult, both with caregivers and inanimate objects. Moreover, when children display consistent problems with interaction, their parents or caregivers may give them fewer opportunities to interact or may act on their behalf more often than they would with a nondisabled child. The result is that a disabled child learns to rely on others to meet his or her needs, a phenomenon known as "learned helplessness." This additional dependence stunts his or her child's cognitive and social development, magnifying whatever problems the child would suffer as a result of the disability. It is important for caregivers to give disabled children frequent opportunities to master new tasks, even when progress seems elusive.

Facial abnormalities

Ankyloglossia (also known as tongue tie) is a congenital anomaly causing limited mobility of the tip of the tongue. This is due to a short and thick frenulum, which attaches the bottom of the tongue to the floor of the mouth. In infants, this condition may effect feeding due to difficulty swallowing and sucking. Later, speech may be affected. However, not all children with ankyloglossia will have articulation deficits. A v-shaped notch at the tip of the tongue, decreased tongue mobility, and tongue protrusion can identify children with this anomaly. Some children will have difficulty producing the lingual phonemes such as (t, d, z, s, θ, ð, n, l). There is controversy whether surgical repair of this condition is necessary.

Oral malocclusions may cause articulation errors. Malocclusions are the misalignment of the upper dental arch (maxilla) and the lower dental arch (mandible). It may also refer to the misalignment of individual teeth. Malocclusions may be inherited as those seen in tooth overcrowding or large spaces between teeth. Accidents and thumb sucking may also be a cause of malocclusions.

Dysarthria

Dysarthria is a mechanical speech disorder caused by injury of the central or peripheral nervous system. Persons with dysarthria typically have deficits in the movement of oral structures and the swallowing mechanism. Speech problems associated with dysarthria are:
- Phonation difficulties of voice quality and voice loudness
- Resonance abnormality, namely hypernasality
- Abnormal prosody, namely monotonous pitch and improper speech rate
- Abnormal articulation with slurred speech, voicing errors, and difficulty with fricatives and affricatives.

Therapy consists of the strengthening of muscles involved in speech, breath control, and speed control. Clients may improve with speech drills, modeling, and phonetic placement. Prosthetic devices or computer-aided devices may be used in severe cases.

Apraxia

Apraxia is a disorder in motor planning and voluntary speech movements due to central nervous system injury. There is no motor weakness or muscular disorder present. The congenital form of apraxia found in children is called Developmental Apraxia of Speech. Acquired apraxia can affect a person of any age.

Therapy is essential in recovery, especially in children. One-on-one therapy is important and my include speech movement sequencing, speech imitation, and speed control. The use of pictures to expand vocabulary is helpful. Sign language can be used to enhance oral language and reduce frustration. Therapist often use touch cueing and physical prompting.

- Children often make great efforts to speak while having difficulty in placing sounds and syllables in correct order. Consonant, vowel, and word cluster errors are seen.
- Articulation errors are inconsistent.
- Incorrect use of speech prosody, whereby the correct use of speech rhythm and infections are improper.
- Ability to understand language is present.
- Spelling and reading difficulties may be present.
- Speech sounds are prolonged and repetitious.
- Children have problems with phonation and resonance.
- Children may have other problems related to motor coordination such as feeding and may not be able to copy mouth movement or sounds proficiently.

Apraxia of speech is characterized by the inability to create meaningful language due to lack of voluntary coordination of the oral structures that produce speech. There is a deficit in the synchronization of the muscles rather than of muscle strength. This coordination deficit is inconsistent. This disorder may be acquired or developmental. Acquired apraxia is typically due to damage to the speech areas of the brain (notably the dominant hemisphere), especially those areas that control motor planning. Causes of acquired apraxia include stroke, trauma, and neurological diseases such as Alzheimer's and myasthenia gravis. In developmental apraxia, the cause is unknown and boys are more often affected than girls. Patients with this disorder have difficulty placing syllables and words in the correct order; therefore they produce slow, choppy speech, with poor prosody. Given that patients with apraxia are aware of their disorder, they often appear to be struggling to produce the correct word and phrases.

Articulation-phonation disorders

The motor-based approaches to the treatment of articulation and phonation disorders presume that children have motor and perceptual defects with regard to speech sound production. These approaches are best used with children who have only several errors in phoneme production; do not have severe articulation deficits; and whose articulation disorder is based on physical insufficiencies.

The most frequently used motor-based approaches are:
- Van Riper's traditional approach
- McCabe and Bradley's multiple phoneme approach
- Baker and Ryan's Monterey Articulation Program
- McDonald's Sensory Approach
- Irwin and Weston's Paired Stimuli Approach

Therapy

Van Riper's traditional approach emphasizes phonetic placement (teaching sounds of phonemes by instruction, modeling and physical guidance), auditory discrimination/perceptual training (teaching the distinction between correct and incorrect speech sounds), and repetition of isolated speech sounds.

McCabe and Bradley's multiple phoneme approach is based on Van Riper's traditional approach except that more than one speech sound is addressed and all problematic speech sounds are addressed in each session. Three phases are employed:

1. Establishment of the correct sound in response to a symbol for that sound.
2. Transfer of target sounds to different situations.
3. Maintenance of accuracy of sound production in various situations and conversation.

Articulation program

Baker and Ryan's Monterey Articulation Program involves programmed conditioning to treat articulation disorders. This approach is based on behavioral therapy principles that speech sounds are learned motor behaviors. Sounds are targeted via a program of steps. These targeted sounds are then generalized to home and classroom, and finally maintenance therapy is employed. Since repetition of motor skills is emphasized, the approach is best for children requiring a structured motor-articulation program.

Sensory approach

McDonald's Sensory Approach involves speech training at the level of the syllable and not the phoneme. Perceptual training is not emphasized but the phonetic environment is important. Practice begins with bi-syllabic and tri-syllabic sounds that are not in error. Correct pronunciation of sounds that are in error are trained and then moved to more varied contexts and then to natural communication.

Paired stimuli approach

Irwin and Weston's Paired Stimuli Approach utilizes words already in the child's vocabulary. An articulation error sound is targeted. Four key words are created, two with the target sound in the initial position and two with the targeted sound in the final position. Ten pictures that suggest words with the targeted sound are selected corresponding to each key word. The key words are arranged around the target word and the child says the key word, the target word, and the key word again. (Training String)

The child must master the pronunciation 9 out of 10 times without reinforcement before moving to the next sound.

Schizophrenia

Schizophrenia, one of the most crippling forms of mental illness, exists when an individual loses the unity of his or her mind, and suffers impaired function in almost every mental area. An individual suffering from schizophrenia may see or hear things that do not exist, may believe that an external force is putting thoughts into their head or controlling their behavior, or may suffer delusions about their identity. Many schizophrenics will develop severe anxieties and will become obsessive about protecting themselves. For most individuals, antipsychotic drugs can help to restore mental control and minimize delusional episodes. However, these drugs can cause a person to become apathetic, and many impoverished individuals will lack the resources to receive treatment at all.

Dementia

Dementia is a slowly progressive decline in cognitive functioning, such that memory, language, and intellectual abilities are impaired. Patients with this syndrome have poor judgment and lose the ability to think abstractly. Later in the condition, patients may suffer hallucinations, delusional thinking, or depression. Language becomes non-fluent, comprehension declines, and patients have difficulty word finding. There is a sharp rise in the prevalence of dementia with advancing age. At ages 65-70, 1.4 % of the population has dementia. This prevalence doubles as age increases. Dementia has dozens of causes but the most common include: Alzheimer's disease, vascular dementia — caused by blockages of small arteries in the brain, frontotemporal dementia, tumors, alcohol/substance abuse, injury, infections (HIV, Jakob-Creutzfeldt disease), neuro-degenerative diseases (e. g. Parkinson's disease).

Neuro-degenerative causes
Alzheimer's disease accounts for up to 70% of all causes of dementias. The histological deficit found in these patients is the deposition of protein in the cortical areas of the brain. These patients first present with mild to moderate short-term memory loss with slow progression. Many patients retain their long-term memory. Their ability to perform activities of daily living becomes hampered by loss of intellectual ability, decreased visual spatial perception, and loss of language fluency.

Parkinson's disease results from a disruption in the conduction of the neurotransmitter dopamine within the basal ganglia. Patients with this disease first display movement abnormalities such as poor balance, slow gait, muscle rigidity, slow speech, difficulty swallowing, and tremor. Dementia occurs in the later stages of the disease.

Huntington's is a genetic disease caused by the degeneration of neurons in the frontal lobe and basal ganglia. These patients display motor deficits typical of uncontrolled, jerky movements (chorea). Speech is slurred and slow. Dementia is an end-stage result.

Frontotemporal Dementia (Pick's Disease) is caused by degeneration of cells in the frontal temporal lobes. The deficits are similar to Alzheimer's with the addition of personality changes and often the complete loss of speech.

Assessment and management

It is important to differentiate reversible causes of dementia from permanent ones. Patients should undergo a full medical screening by a healthcare professional to rule out treatable causes of dementia. Medical screening includes a thorough medical and social history and pertinent diagnostic tests. It is important to assess the patient's orientation to person, place, and time as well as the ability to recognize familiar people, objects, and place. Also included in the assessment of patients with dementia are their memory, ability to abstract, awareness of spatial relationships, expressive and receptive language, ability to calculate, and ability to perform activities of daily living. Also important is the assessment of mobility and swallowing. A psychological evaluation may also be appropriate. Treatment is based on individual needs and my include speech therapy, physical therapy, safety training, medications, and psychosocial counseling. Family members should play a large part in treatment strategies. Modification of the patient's environment to improve safety and orientation is extremely important.

Behavior genetics

The science of the interrelationships between behavior, heredity, and environment is known as behavior genetics. Specifically, behavior genetics is the study of how differences between people are determined by these factors. Perhaps the most famous experiments in behavior genetics are those related to twins and adopted children. Behavior geneticists often take a look at identical and fraternal twins, to see whether there are differences in behavior between individuals with identical chromosomes. Of special interest are cases in which twins were separated at birth and raised in starkly different environments. In adoption studies, meanwhile, behavior geneticists examine whether adopted children demonstrate the influence of their genes or of the environment in which they grew up. Again, the best cases for examination are often those in which one sibling is adopted and raised in a different environment.

Chromosomal abnormalities

When a human being has too many or too few chromosomes, he may display particular tendencies. For instance, if a person has an extra chromosome 21, he will have Down syndrome, which manifests as physical deformity and intellectual disabilities. Males with an extra X chromosome have Klinefelter's syndrome, which is linked to physical abnormalities. Females with a missing X chromosome have Turner syndrome, which manifests as intellectual disabilities, physical abnormalities, and shortness. Males with an extra Y chromosome have XYY syndrome, which tends to make them exceptionally tall.

Gene-linked abnormalities

There are more than 7000 diseases and abnormalities that are thought to be caused by genetic issues. These conditions range in severity. For instance, many African-Americans suffer from sickle-cell anemia, a blood disorder that prevents the effective distribution of oxygen. Genetic abnormalities are also to blame for diabetes, in which the body produces insufficient insulin and has a hard time regulating blood-sugar levels. Another genetic abnormality is tied to cystic fibrosis, which causes glandular malfunction, digestive problems, and clogged respiratory passageways. A classic genetic abnormality is hemophilia, in which blood fails to clot properly. If left untreated, hemophilia can be fatal. Other common genetic abnormalities include Huntington's disease, Tay-Sachs disease, spina bifida, and phenylketonuria.

Giftedness

A gifted person will score at least 130 on an intelligence test, or will demonstrate some special talent in a particular field. A gifted child will often come up with unique solutions to problems. Gifted children do not need as much guidance, because they tend to be self-motivated when it comes to their education. This is particularly true when a gifted child has a narrow area of interest, like science, music, or books. For the most part, gifted children are well adjusted socially, and do not have any mental abnormalities.

Learning disabilities

In 2004, the United States passed legislation defining learning disabilities as "disorders in one or more of the basic psychological processes involved in understanding or in using language, spoken or written, which may manifest itself in an imperfect ability to listen, think, speak, read, write, spell, or do mathematical calculations." There are a number of learning disabilities diagnosed and managed in the contemporary classroom. In particular, though, teachers focus on learning disabilities that relate to the acquisition of academic knowledge. It is important to remember that learning-disabled people are not less intelligent, and usually do not have other physical, social, or mental impairments.

Diagnosis
Learning disabilities can be hard to diagnose, but they are most likely present when a student's level of achievement in school is two or more grade levels lower than the ability he has demonstrated on a standardized IQ tests. The federal government has issued loose guidelines for the determination of learning disability, although states and local school systems are responsible for specific procedures of diagnosis and treatment. Some students are considered learning-disabled by one jurisdiction but not by others. At all times, it is important to enlist the help of doctors and child psychologists in making a diagnosis of learning disability.

Effects of diagnosis
For some children, a diagnosis of learning disability creates a stigma, or a false impression that academic success is impossible. However, once a child is diagnosed with a learning disability, it becomes easier for him to obtain useful academic services, like tutoring and specialized instruction. Also, the diagnosis of a learning disability may improve a child's self-esteem if he perceives that once seemingly insurmountable problems can be treated and overcome. However, some children are teased or alienated from their peers after they

receive the diagnosis. Also, students who have been diagnosed with learning disabilities may be held to a lower standard by teachers.

Causes

As of yet, the causes of learning disability have not been identified. Some researchers believe that learning disabilities like dyslexia are based on genetics. The precise gene that transmits these learning disabilities, however, has not been identified. Magnetic resonance imaging (MRI) and positron emission tomography (PET) scans suggest that certain regions of the brain, like the thalamus, exhibit characteristic behavior in learning-disabled people. The thalamus is responsible for directing information from the sense organs to various parts of the brain.

Dyslexia

Dyslexia is one of the more common learning disabilities. It is characterized by an inability to recognize written words. For a long time, researchers believed that dyslexia was associated with vision problems, but it is now assumed that the disorder has more to do with speech and hearing abnormalities. Specifically, brain scans indicate that dyslexics have unusual structures in the language area of the cerebral cortex's left hemisphere. Contrary to what may be assumed, individuals with dyslexia typically have average or better than average intelligence. Overwhelmingly, dyslexia afflicts males rather than females. The best treatment for dyslexia is remedial education.

Intellectual disabilities

Intellectual disabilities can have organic or cultural-familial causes. The organic causes of intellectual disabilities include Down syndrome, Turner syndrome, brain damage, fragile X syndrome, prenatal exposure to alcohol or drugs, environmental toxins, and malnutrition. The cultural-familial causes of intellectual disabilities are heredity and an unstimulating living environment. Some psychologists think that individuals who score between 50 and 70 on intelligence tests and who do not have brain damage may just be at the lower end of the normal distribution of IQ scores for the population.

Major depression

A major depression is an overwhelming feeling of sadness that extends over a long period of time. Though about one in ten Americans will experience a major depression in any given year, only about one in every three of these will seek treatment. Most cases of depression can be helped with psychotherapy, medication, or both. An individual may be depressed of he or she feels sad or discouraged for a long period, lacks energy, has difficulty concentrating, continually thinks of death or suicide, withdraws from his or her social life, has no interest in sex, or has a major change in his or her eating or sleeping habits. Some individuals who do not respond to therapy or medication may receive electroconvulsive therapy, the administration of electrical current through electrodes placed on the scalp.

Manic depression (bipolar disorder)

Individuals suffering from manic depression will have violent mood swings, ranging from unbridled euphoria to crushing despair. An individual with this form of mental illness may also have wild, uncontrollable thoughts, unrealistic self-confidence, difficulty concentrating, delusions, hallucinations, and odd changes in behavior. During a "high," such an individual may make unrealistic and grandiose plans, or take dangerous risks. During a "low" period, the same individual will feel hopeless, and may contemplate suicide. Manic depression, otherwise known as bipolar disorder, is a very serious disorder that requires immediate medical treatment. Anti-convulsants and lithium carbonate are the most common drugs prescribed to treat this illness.

Adjustment disorder

An adjustment disorder is an abnormally pronounced reaction to the stress of life, particularly the stresses associated with major changes like entering school, getting married, or having a child. Some people are very susceptible to adjustment disorder, which can manifest as anxiety, depression, or erratic behavior. If left unaddressed, adjustment disorders can last for months or even years. Perhaps even worse, adjustment disorders can prevent people from making necessary life changes in the first place. The result is stagnation and further anxiety and depression. Most experts recommend counseling and psychotherapy for people suffering from adjustment disorder. This condition is often rooted in a negative experience from the individual's past, and a resolution of this past event can eliminate the adjustment disorder in the present.

PTSD

Post-traumatic stress disorder (PTSD) occurs in those who have endured a prolonged or especially acute trauma, such as war, rape, or natural disaster. In the past, PTSD often went by the name "shell shock." A person suffering from PTSD will appear depressed, and he or she may be unable to move past the traumatic incident mentally without medical intervention. PTSD usually manifests within six months of the trauma. A person with this condition will be unable to concentrate, interact meaningfully with others, or function professionally. Over time, PTSD can have a deleterious effect on memory and cognition. For young people, PTSD can impair mental and social development. There are a number of useful treatments for the condition, including medication, psychotherapy, and cognitive therapy. If left untreated, PTSD can get worse and further impede development.

Important terms

- Culture: The set of attitudes, behaviors, ideas, and beliefs that predominate among a group of people, as well as the physical acts, institutions, gestures, and manners of expression that are acceptable in that group.
- Ethnic identity: The feeling of identification and belonging with people from a particular background, including a sense of solidarity with the culture and traditions of those people.
- Socialization: The process of acquiring the cultural artifacts (values, behaviors, beliefs, etc.) of a society in order to integrate oneself.
- Independent variable: The variable in an experiment that is manipulated. In other words, the variable that is changed to see what effects that change will have on the system. Often referred to as Factor X.
- Dependent variable: The variable in an experiment that changes as a result of the manipulation of the independent variable. Often referred to as Factor Y.

- Extraneous variable: Any factors besides the independent and dependent variables that can have an effect on the results of a research study. For instance, the environmental conditions in which the experiment is performed, the health and education of the subjects, and the time of day at which this experiment is conducted.
- Cohort: A group of people with one demographic factor in common. For instance, a group of people born during a particular interval, or in a particular location.
- Random sample: A representative group of members from a population selected by some method that gave every member of the population the same chance of being selected.
- Control group: All of the members of an experiment who are not affected by the independent variable. The data generated by the control group is compared with the data generated by the group in which the independent variable is manipulated.
- Zygote: Fertilized egg cell (ovum).
- Blastocyst: Collection of cells made by cell division during the first week of a pregnancy. The embryo will be formed with an inner layer composed of the blastocyst.
- Trophoblast: Outside layer of cells on the blastocyst, which helps connect it to the wall of the uterus. The trophoblast will ultimately develop into the placenta.
- Embryo: The fetus from the time at which it attaches to the wall of the uterus until the end of the eighth week of pregnancy, when it can be recognized as human.
- Axon: Long, thin nerve fibers that extend out from a neuron, and along which information is transmitted. Many axons are covered in a myelin sheath, and may have at the ends terminal buttons, from which neurotransmitters flow into the synapses between neurons.
- Dendrite: A fiber projecting out from a cell body towards other cells. Typically has a number of branches.
- Neuron: Nerve cell that helps to communicate information around the body. The neurons in the brain process and transmit information. Nerves are ropey bundles of neurons.
- Synapse: The gap between the axon of one neuron and the dendrites of another, over which information is transmitted. Nerve cells don't come into physical contact, but are separated by synaptic gaps, across which neurotransmitter chemicals carry information.
- Myelination: The process in which a collection of fat cells encase an axon. These fat cells are called myelin, and they lubricate electrical transmissions, insulate the axon, and are believed to generate energy for the neuron.
- Sex: Male or female physical characteristics, specifically those related to reproduction.
- Gender: Social and psychological characteristics related to being a male or female. Composed of what a given culture or society believes to be masculine or feminine characteristics.
- Gender identity: A person's self-image as it relates to masculinity or femininity. In other words, the extent to which a person perceives himself as masculine or feminine.
- Gender roles: The beliefs and expectations a society or culture has for males and females.
- Phonology: System of sounds in a language, including the combination of sounds to create words. A phoneme is the smallest sound unit. There are 42 phonemes in English.

- Morphology: A language's rules for creating words. Words are made up of morphemes, which are the smallest sensible units of language.
- Syntax: The rules by which words must be ordered in a language in order to produce sensible sentences and phrases.
- Semantics: The meanings or definitions of words.
- Pragmatics: The alteration or adjustment of language for particular situations or contexts.
- Reflexive smile: Unprompted by stimuli. For instance, the smile that passes over the face of a sleeping infant.
- Social smile: Prompted by external stimuli, as for instance a familiar face or voice. Two-month-olds may demonstrate social smiling.
- Stranger anxiety: Fear of unfamiliar people. Typically does not manifest until between six months and a year.
- Separation protest: The cries of an infant forced to part ways with a caregiver.
- Grief: A state of sadness following the death of a friend or family member. A grieving individual is often numb and empty, and may vacillate between sadness and rage. During grief, a person is likely to experience intense yearning for the deceased.
- Prolonged grief: An extremely long bout of grief, characterized by numbness or detachment, and endured by between 10 and 20% of those who lose a loved one. In prolonged grief, the person often feels negative about life in general, and may become physically and mentally depressed.
- Bereavement: The time immediately following the death of a loved one. The people left behind are called the bereaved, and are likely to be grieving. Different cultures have different expectations for the behavior and conduct of the bereaved.
- Mourning: The cultural practices related to behavior after the death of a loved one. Some common gestures of mourning are wailing, wearing black, holding a funeral, and chanting. Many cultures have very specific requirements for mourning. For instance, some cultures insist on cremation, while burial is the norm in others.
- Microsystem: The network of social ties in a person's life, as for instance family, friends, and colleagues. Also, the physical environment in which those ties exist.
- Mesosystem: The manner in which a person's microsystems interact. For instance, the relationship between a person's work environment and their family life.
- Exosystem: All of the social mechanisms that affect a person's behavior. For example, relationships based on religious affiliation can affect behavior at work.
- Macrosystem: The general culture in which a person lives, including the prevailing economic, political, religious, and social mores.

Practice Test

Practice Questions

1. A correlative method of studying child behavior indicates what type of question?
   a. which comes first?
   b. what goes with what?
   c. who did what?
   d. why did that happen?

2. Time sampling is a type of...
   a. systematic observation.
   b. semi-clinical interview.
   c. sondage.
   d. spontaneous conviction.

3. According to Piaget, when a child's answer to a question is the result of careful thought, it can be termed...
   a. romancing.
   b. suggested conviction.
   c. answers at random.
   d. liberated conviction.

4. Children who are very susceptible to external stimuli, may be called what?
   a. field dependent
   b. field independent
   c. externally dependent
   d. internally impaired

5. What was the focus of Jean Piaget's theory of development?
   a. physiological development
   b. speech development
   c. cognitive development
   d. psychosocial development

6. Which of the following theorists focused primarily on psychosocial development?
   a. B.F. Skinner
   b. Sigmund Freud
   c. Erik Erikson
   d. Jean Piaget

7. What does the "cultural drift hypothesis" address?
   a. effect rather than cause
   b. cause rather than effect
   c. neither cause nor effect
   d. both cause and effect

- 99 -

8. If a research project involves naturalistic observation, does the researcher need to obtain informed consent from the subjects involved?
    a. no, consent is never needed with naturalistic observation
    b. yes, informed consent must always be obtained
    c. yes, but only if it can be obtained without the subject's knowledge of the type of research being done.
    d. no, if the research can be reasonably assumed to not be harmful

9. When does the blastocyst period take place?
    a. from fertilization until the fifteenth week of development
    b. from the third week until the eighth week of development
    c. from the tenth week until the twelfth week of development
    d. from fertilization until approximately the fifteenth day of development

10. A fontanelle is...
    a. an early development in the first stage of pregnancy.
    b. an irregular indentation at the base of an infant's skull.
    c. the soft spot on the top of an infant's head.
    d. a treatment used for PKU after birth.

11. What is lallation?
    a. repetitive sounds a child makes
    b. the process of a mother producing human milk
    c. a treatment modality for new mothers
    d. the initial stage of speech development

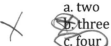

12. Which of the following are female sex hormones?
    a. progesterone and estrogen
    b. testosterone and progesterone
    c. androgens and estrogen
    d. estrogen and testosterone

13. According to Masters & Johnson, how many stages of sexual response are there?
    a. two
    b. three
    c. four
    d. five

14. What function of the nervous system keeps the body in balance?
    a. peripheral adjustments
    b. somatic responses
    c. homeostasis
    d. cerebellum

15. The pinna, meatus and malleus are parts of which sensory organ?
    a. the skin
    b. the mouth
    c. the eyes
    d. the ear

16. The cephalocaudal principle refers to the idea that...
     a. development progresses from head to toe.
     b. development progresses from toe to head.
     c. development is a complex process.
     d. development is a time-intensive process.

17. According to Elisabeth Kubler-Ross' stages of death and dying, most people go through how many stages in dealing with imminent death?
     a. two
     b. three
     c. four
     d. five

18. Disengagement theory says that an elderly individual will be happiest if he...
     a. keeps as active as possible.
     b. gradually withdraws from life.
     c. forms many personal relationships.
     d. learns new things.

19. Eric Lenneberg, a proponent of the "critical-period" theory of language development, believed that language development correlated less with age and more with...
     a. critical-sensation acquisition.
     b. visual acuity.
     c. motor development.
     d. I.Q.

20. Which of the following would be associated with learning theory?
     a. Watson
     b. Freud
     c. Rogers
     d. Alberts

21. Memory operates using three basic steps. Which of the following is the first step?
     a. encoding
     b. storage
     c. transfer
     d. retrieval

22. Which of the following is a type of sensory memory specifically involving vision?
     a. echoic memory
     b. long-term memory
     c. iconic memory
     d. short-term memory

23. Dyslexia is a...
     a. developmental reading disorder.
     b. developmental writing disorder.
     c. developmental attention disorder.
     d. developmental arithmetic disorder.

24. If a child demonstrates impulsivity, inattention and hyperactivity, he may be diagnosed with which of the following?
   a. ADHD
   b. dyslexia
   c. dysgraphia
   d. dyscalculia

25. In information processing, an individual uses a rule of thumb to reach a conclusion. To what does this type of problem solving refer?
   a. evaluation
   b. an algorithm
   c. a heuristic
   d. production

26. A child watches her mother drying dishes. She picks up a towel and cup, and begins to dry the dish as well. Which type of behavior might this indicate?
   a. cognitive map
   b. biofeedback
   c. self-reinforcement
   d. modeling   Bandura

27. A toddler is praised by her mother each time she puts her toys back in her toy chest, so she continues to put her toys away each night. Which type of learning is this?
   a. operant conditioning
   b. classical conditioning
   c. cognitive learning
   d. Pavlovian

28. Stimulus generalization is...   Pavlov
   a. a Pavlovian concept.
   b. a Freudian concept.
   c. a Bandura construct.
   d. a Rogerian therapy technique.

29. Extinction refers to eliminating a behavior through...
   a. positive stimuli.
   b. aversive stimuli.
   c. removing a reinforcement.
   d. reinforcement.

30. Even though he has never been trained in CPR, a young man saves the life of someone who has collapsed by using the basic CPR techniques. This is most likely an example of...
   a. a very high I.Q.
   b. heroic tendencies.
   c. latent learning.
   d. symbiotic association.

31. Janie has watched her mother knit for years. One day she decides to try knitting, and is surprised to discover that she is able to knit. Which type of learning might this be called?
    a. observational learning
    b. latent learning
    c. symbiotic association
    d. biofeedback learning

32. In what might an electromyography, electroencephalograph and blood pressure cuff be used?
    a. Rogerian intervention
    b. intensive psychotherapy
    c. hypnotherapy
    d. biofeedback

33. When an individual believes that nothing they do can affect what happens to them or their environment, it is called...
    a. observational learning.
    b. learned helplessness.
    c. learned ineffectiveness.
    d. inability to thrive.

34. In terms of memory, "clustering" refers to...
    a. placing information into higher order categories.
    b. placing information into lower order categories.
    c. organizing information according to alphabet only.
    d. organizing information according to color only.

35. Children achieve "conservation" during which Piaget stage?
    a. formal operational
    b. sensorimotor
    c. concrete operations
    d. preoperational

36. A child's first spoken words conveying a complete thought are called...
    a. motherese.
    b. telegraphic speech.
    c. alliteration.
    d. holophrases

37. What is a "language acquisition device"? Noam Chomsky
    a. our inborn ability to acquire language
    b. a standard treatment for dyslexia
    c. a machine used to aid children with developmental problems
    d. a technique to minimize stuttering

38. Which is a type of language commonly used between mother and child?
    a. MLU
    b. LAD
    c. motherese
    d. alliteration

- 103 -

39. A barrier to problem solving discussed by Karl Duncker is called what?
    a. heuristic
    b. algorithm
    c. functional fixedness
    d. evaluation

40. According to Teresa Amabile's analysis of research on creativity, which of the following can make a person more creative?
    a. intrinsic motivation
    b. a high-paying job
    c. parenthood
    d. a stress-free life

41. What is aphasia?
    a. a visual deficit
    b. an auditory disability
    c. a language disturbance
    d. a mobility issue

42. To what does "androgynous" refer?
    a. a balance of both masculine and feminine characteristics
    b. a predominantly feminine individual
    c. a predominantly masculine individual
    d. a male with more feminine qualities than is the norm

43. The theory that how we think is affected by our choice of the language we use is called...
    a. a language acquisition device.
    b. the linguistic-relativity hypothesis. → wharfian hypothesis
    c. nativism.
    d. language resemblance.

44. When thoughts and actions are incompatible, it is called...
    a. a semantic differential.
    b. cognitive consistency.
    c. an inferiority complex.
    d. cognitive dissonance.

45. Piaget's concept of "imminent justice" referred to...
    a. the court system's response to adolescent criminal behavior.
    b. adult female moral aptitude.
    c. the moral attitude of adult males.
    d. the moral development of children.

46. Which of the following states are believed to be the healthiest?
    a. single
    b. legally separated
    c. married
    d. widowed

47. A ten-year-old, upon the birth of a baby brother, begins sleeping with his baby blankie again. What might this behavior be called?
   a. regression
   b. repression
   c. projection
   d. sublimation

48. Sigmund Freud theorized that the id...
   a. was our common sense.
   b. operates on the "perfection principle."
   c. was our moral taskmaster.
   d. represented our basic needs.

49. Freud said that gender identity is a result of...
   a. identification with the same sex parent.
   b. identification with the same sex peer group.
   c. the id.
   d. instinct.

50. What do social learning theorists say causes aggression?
   a. rewards and punishments only
   b. rewards, punishments and society
   c. society only
   d. internalized factors only

Answer Key and Explanations

1. B: Correlative methods try to determine which variables go together. Such a method seeks to make connections, such as "at what age do children first make eye contact regularly?" or "how many words do children speak at a given age?" The correlation coefficient can range from -1.00 to +1.00, and the outcome of a correlational study is either positive, negative or has no correlation.

2. A: Time sampling is a type of systematic observation that involves the researcher noting the number of times a particular behavior occurs within a given time frame. There are different types of time sampling, including momentary time sampling (MTS) and partial interval (PI) sampling.

3. D: Piaget describes answers that are from the depths of the child's mind as liberated conviction. These are very useful types of responses. On the other hand, romancing (making up an answer without thinking), suggested conviction (answers to please the researcher) and answers at random, are three types of reply that are of little value.

4. A: Field dependent and field independent are cognitive styles. A field independent child might be said to be able to deal with distracting, external stimuli more effectively than the field dependent child, who is significantly affected by external distractions.

5. C: Jean Piaget focused on cognitive development, and formulated a series of four stages to explain a child's level of ability at certain age ranges. The stages are sensorimotor, preoperational, concrete operations and formal operations. He also focused on the role of maturation and experience in a child's development.

6. C: Erikson was a psychoanalyst who developed the only major theory that covered normal human development and also took into account the entire human lifespan. He formulated eight stages of development, each of which is dependant upon the resolution of a crisis. His stages are "basic trust vs. basic mistrust", "autonomy vs. shame and doubt", "initiative vs. guilt", "industry vs. inferiority", "identity vs. role confusion", "intimacy vs. isolation", "generativity vs. stagnation" and "basic integrity vs. basic despair."

7. A: The cultural drift hypothesis considers the possibility that one particular variable may be the effect of another variable, rather than the assumed cause. For example, individuals with lower than average intellectual abilities may often be seen in a lower socioeconomic class. One might assume that the intellectual level is caused by the economic conditions in which the person lives. However, cultural drift hypothesis would suggest that those with low intellectual ability may "drift" toward the lower socioeconomic status, making the economic situation an effect of the lower intellect.

8. D: Put simply, you can dispense with informed consent if the research won't cause harm, or where permitted by law or the regulations of the institution. Within these simple guidelines are more specific specifications, but those are the general considerations.

9. D: The zygote produces cells and moves down the fallopian tubes until it eventually attaches itself to the uterine wall. The zygote then produces structures, such as the chorion, to provide nourishment and growth.

10. C: An infant's bones are softer and shaped differently at birth than those of an adult. The fontanelle is a soft spot on the top of an infant's head where the bones of the skull are not yet fully fused together. The bones will fuse together between nine months and a year of age, forming a completely hard skullcap.

11. A: At around six to eight months of age, the child enters into a late stage of babbling, and progresses from there to making repetitive sounds, such as ba-ba, la-la, and ma-ma. This repetitive vocalization is termed lallation, which includes both vowel and consonant sounds. This type of behavior shows the child's progress at making sounds that are a more focused attempt at direct communication.

12. A: The two major female sex hormones are progesterone and estrogen. Both have been linked specifically to sexual arousal in animals, and the human female may be more likely to be interested in sexual intercourse when levels of the hormones are at their highest. Androgens and testosterone are both male sex hormones.

13. C: Masters & Johnson were a pioneering team in researching human sexuality. They identified four stages of sexual response based on vasocongestion (blood flow), and myotonia (muscle contraction). The four stages are excitement, plateau, orgasm and resolution. A number of identified behaviors have been detailed for each of these stages, and difficulties can arise at any time during the four stages because of a number of factors.

14. C: Homeostasis refers to an assortment of automatic adjustments to important bodily functions by the autonomic nervous system. It ensures the "balance" that is necessary for survival. For example, when the body gets too hot, it begins to sweat. If the temperature turns cold, the body begins to shiver. Adjustments are made all the time to keep the body in equilibrium.

15. D: The pinna refers to the outer ear, the meatus (or "auditory meatus") is the ear canal, and the malleus is the "hammer" (the bone that is nudged when the eardrum vibrates). Each of these is a part of the auditory/hearing sense.

16. A: The cephalocaudal principle refers to the idea that development progresses from head to toe. In other words, development begins with the upper parts of the body, and later moves to the lower parts of the body.

17. D: Elizabeth Kubler-Ross, a pioneer in the study of death and dying, said there are five stages an individual commonly goes through in coming to terms with imminent death. Those stages are denial, anger, bargaining, depression, and acceptance.

18. B: Disengagement theory says that people will be happier at the end of their lives if they gradually disengage from it. In other words, this theory would recommend that an elderly individual involve himself in fewer activities, spend more time alone, and minimize personal relationships.

19. C: Lenneberg felt that motor development was a good indicator of maturity level, and thus correlated better with language development than the chronological age of the individual.

20. A: John B. Watson is often called the "father of behaviorism" and is associated with learning theory. He was the first to study the effect of learning on behavior. He felt that only those behaviors that are observable, rather than thoughts and feelings, are significant.

21. A: Encoding is the first step in how memory works, and is the process of putting information into some meaningful order. There are a number of ways to do this, such as encoding by sound or meaning, or making associations between new material and previously remembered information. The second step to memory is storage (to make sure the material stays in memory), and retrieval (the ability to get the material out of storage).

22. C: The type of sensory memory that specifically involves vision is called iconic memory. Iconic memory, just as it sounds, is memory of what you see. It is not as enduring as echoic memory, which is a memory of information obtained through the sense of hearing.

23. A: Dyslexia is a developmental reading disorder most often characterized by reading difficulties as well as trouble differentiating particular sounds in verbal language. A common symptom is the reversal of letters and numbers when writing. General disorganization and memory issues are among some of the other symptoms one might see with a dyslexia diagnosis.

24. A: Attention Deficit Hyperactivity Disorder (ADHD) is one of the more common of the childhood disorders. A child with ADHD may have difficulty focusing and maintaining attention, become easily confused, be late with school assignments, be impatient and constantly in motion, as well as exhibiting other possible symptoms.

25. C: Unlike an algorithm, which is a strategy by which the individual tries every possible way to find the answer to a problem, the heuristic is far more limited. With a heuristic approach, a general rule of thumb is used to reach the solution. A heuristic approach may find an answer more quickly than the algorithm, but while quicker (when it's effective), it may not find the answer at all.

26. D: Modeling is a type of observational learning, and according to Bandura, consists of four basic steps. Those steps include perceiving the significant details of the behavior, remembering the behavior, converting the perceived information into action, and being motivated to engage in the behavior. Modeling can be a big influence on behavior and is also used in therapeutic approaches.

27. A: Operant conditioning is a type of associative learning that involves the consequences of the behavior. If the consequences of the behavior are positive, then the behavior is likely to be repeated. If the consequences of the behavior are negative, then the likelihood is that the behavior will not be repeated.

28. A: Sometimes a conditioned response is transferred to a stimulus that is similar to, but not the same as, the stimulus originally paired with the unconditioned one. This is an associative learning concept that came out of Pavlov's work with classical conditioning.

29. C: Extinction means eliminating a previous behavior. It is accomplished by no longer reinforcing a response, but can also be accomplished via punishment. An intermittently reinforced behavior will take longer to extinguish than a continually reinforced behavior. Likewise, a fixed reinforcement schedule is easier than a variable one.

30. C: Latent learning describes a type of learning that is not evident until the individual is properly motivated to exhibit it. In our example, the young man may not have even realized he knew how to do CPR, but just from seeing others do it or hearing about it, he was able to react appropriately in an emergency situation.

31. A: As in our example, people can learn by simply watching others do something. Imitating what one observes another person doing has been shown to be effective in the development of many types of behavior, including children learning simple social behaviors and aggressive behavior.

32. D: In biofeedback, people learn to recognize and control their own physiological processes. It develops an enhanced awareness of what one's body is doing and how outside influences affect the body. The aids/machines used in biofeedback can be used to inform the individual of changes in brain activity, muscle contractions and blood pressure among other factors.

33. B: Learned helplessness is the belief that the self or one's environment cannot be affected by what the individual does. The term is used in relation to both animals and humans. An outcome of this belief system is that the individual, without the motivation to try, does not learn any responses that can affect change.

34. A: An example would be someone who had to remember a list of several animals, and as an aid to memory, clusters all the dogs into one group and all the cats into another. Individuals who cluster information are more likely to remember it accurately at a later time.

35. C: Conservation refers to the ability to know that something remains the same even though its appearance may change. Piaget believed that this is not achieved in children until the concrete operational stage, which takes place from age seven to eleven.

36. D: A sound made by the child that can have several meanings, but is interpreted at the time it is uttered to convey a particular message, is called a holophrase. Holophrases are the first spoken words and can communicate a complete thought in just one word.

37. A: A language acquisition device was theorized by Noam Chomsky. He said that the human brain is constructed in such a way that it gives humans the ability to talk in much the same way as they are naturally able to learn to walk.

38. C: Motherese is a type of language often used between mother and child. Using fewer pronouns and verbs, repeating key ideas and raising the pitch of the voice, are a few characteristics of "motherese". In order to develop fluent language skills, children need to have adults speak to them, and therefore motherese can be an important part of language development.

39. C: Functional fixedness happens when an individual relies too heavily on previously used ways of dealing with problems. This overreliance inhibits the ability to reach novel solutions, and therefore makes problem solving more difficult.

40. A: Amabile's review found six factors that can enhance creativity in an individual. Those six factors are intrinsic motivation (doing something because one wants to), choice, stimulation, inspirational models, freedom from evaluation (no fear of being judged), and independence (no fear of being observed and criticized).

41. C: Aphasias often occur as a result of damage to the brain in the left hemisphere, where language abilities are affected. This can be due to a stroke, head injury or other injury-inducing incidents. The type of aphasia depends upon where exactly in the left hemisphere the damage occurs and the extent of that damage.

42. A: Sandra Bern theorized that the healthiest individual is one who has a balance of the positive, gender stereotyped characteristics of both male and female. When both types of characteristics are well integrated, she calls this person "androgynous."

43. B: The linguistic-relativity hypothesis, sometimes also called the Whorfian hypothesis, theorizes that words do not simply communicate thoughts, but also that they shape those thoughts. Likewise, the use of a different language can alter how one perceives the world.

44. D: Cognitive dissonance occurs when an individual's thoughts and actions are incompatible, or when incompatible opinions are held. This state causes psychological discomfort, which can be eased through change that brings about harmony.

45. D: Piaget explored the concept of imminent justice in relation to the moral development of children. More specifically, imminent justice refers to the tendency of children to believe that if someone is hurt while doing something bad, that negative result is actually "punishment" for the bad behavior.

46. C: Research seems to indicate that people who are married tend to be physically healthier. It may also be that healthier individuals are more likely to marry and stay married. Whichever is the case, it seems that there is a positive correlation between marriage and health.

47. A: Regression is a Freudian defense mechanism, one of several ways in which the individual deals unconsciously with anxiety. In our example, the ten-year-old is likely feeling anxiety over the new addition to the family, and therefore regresses to a previous state where he felt more secure in his position in the family.

48. D: Freud theorized that the personality was composed of three parts, the id, ego and superego. The id represented the basic needs of the individual, such as the need for food and sex. The id operates on the "pleasure principle" and, just as it sounds, refers to the id's demand for immediate gratification of those basic needs.

49. A: Sigmund Freud said that gender identity is the result of identification with the same sex parent, and also due to the child's anatomy. This view is a part of his psychoanalytic theory, and was the first significant attempt to address the issue of gender identity in development.

50. B: Social learning theorists say that people learn to be aggressive for two basic reasons. They learn aggression through a series of rewards and punishments from interaction with others, both inside and outside the home. Societal attitudes also play a part in the acquisition of aggressive behavior through societal views of acceptable levels of aggression.

Secret Key #1 - Time is Your Greatest Enemy

Pace Yourself

Wear a watch. At the beginning of the test, check the time (or start a chronometer on your watch to count the minutes), and check the time after every few questions to make sure you are "on schedule."

If you are forced to speed up, do it efficiently. Usually one or more answer choices can be eliminated without too much difficulty. Above all, don't panic. Don't speed up and just begin guessing at random choices. By pacing yourself, and continually monitoring your progress against your watch, you will always know exactly how far ahead or behind you are with your available time. If you find that you are one minute behind on the test, don't skip one question without spending any time on it, just to catch back up. Take 15 fewer seconds on the next four questions, and after four questions you'll have caught back up. Once you catch back up, you can continue working each problem at your normal pace.

Furthermore, don't dwell on the problems that you were rushed on. If a problem was taking up too much time and you made a hurried guess, it must be difficult. The difficult questions are the ones you are most likely to miss anyway, so it isn't a big loss. It is better to end with more time than you need than to run out of time.

Lastly, sometimes it is beneficial to slow down if you are constantly getting ahead of time. You are always more likely to catch a careless mistake by working more slowly than quickly, and among very high-scoring test takers (those who are likely to have lots of time left over), careless errors affect the score more than mastery of material.

Secret Key #2 - Guessing is not Guesswork

You probably know that guessing is a good idea. Unlike other standardized tests, there is no penalty for getting a wrong answer. Even if you have no idea about a question, you still have a 20-25% chance of getting it right.

Most test takers do not understand the impact that proper guessing can have on their score. Unless you score extremely high, guessing will significantly contribute to your final score.

Monkeys Take the Test

What most test takers don't realize is that to insure that 20-25% chance, you have to guess randomly. If you put 20 monkeys in a room to take this test, assuming they answered once per question and behaved themselves, on average they would get 20-25% of the questions correct. Put 20 test takers in the room, and the average will be much lower among guessed questions. Why?

1. The test writers intentionally write deceptive answer choices that "look" right. A test taker has no idea about a question, so he picks the "best looking" answer, which is often wrong. The monkey has no idea what looks good and what doesn't, so it will consistently be right about 20-25% of the time.
2. Test takers will eliminate answer choices from the guessing pool based on a hunch or intuition. Simple but correct answers often get excluded, leaving a 0% chance of being correct. The monkey has no clue, and often gets lucky with the best choice.

This is why the process of elimination endorsed by most test courses is flawed and detrimental to your performance. Test takers don't guess; they make an ignorant stab in the dark that is usually worse than random.

$5 Challenge

Let me introduce one of the most valuable ideas of this course—the $5 challenge:

You only mark your "best guess" if you are willing to bet $5 on it.
You only eliminate choices from guessing if you are willing to bet $5 on it.

Why $5? Five dollars is an amount of money that is small yet not insignificant, and can really add up fast (20 questions could cost you $100). Likewise, each answer choice on one question of the test will have a small impact on your overall score, but it can really add up to a lot of points in the end.

The process of elimination IS valuable. The following shows your chance of guessing it right:

If you eliminate wrong answer choices until only this many remain:	Chance of getting it correct:
1	100%
2	50%
3	33%

However, if you accidentally eliminate the right answer or go on a hunch for an incorrect answer, your chances drop dramatically—to 0%. By guessing among all the answer choices, you are GUARANTEED to have a shot at the right answer.

That's why the $5 test is so valuable. If you give up the advantage and safety of a pure guess, it had better be worth the risk.

What we still haven't covered is how to be sure that whatever guess you make is truly random. Here's the easiest way:

Always pick the first answer choice among those remaining.

Such a technique means that you have decided, **before you see a single test question**, exactly how you are going to guess, and since the order of choices tells you nothing about which one is correct, this guessing technique is perfectly random.

This section is not meant to scare you away from making educated guesses or eliminating choices; you just need to define when a choice is worth eliminating. The $5 test, along with a pre-defined random guessing strategy, is the best way to make sure you reap all of the benefits of guessing.

Secret Key #3 - Practice Smarter, Not Harder

Many test takers delay the test preparation process because they dread the awful amounts of practice time they think necessary to succeed on the test. We have refined an effective method that will take you only a fraction of the time.

There are a number of "obstacles" in the path to success. Among these are answering questions, finishing in time, and mastering test-taking strategies. All must be executed on the day of the test at peak performance, or your score will suffer. The test is a mental marathon that has a large impact on your future.

Just like a marathon runner, it is important to work your way up to the full challenge. So first you just worry about questions, and then time, and finally strategy:

Success Strategy

1. Find a good source for practice tests.
2. If you are willing to make a larger time investment, consider using more than one study guide. Often the different approaches of multiple authors will help you "get" difficult concepts.
3. Take a practice test with no time constraints, with all study helps, "open book." Take your time with questions and focus on applying strategies.
4. Take a practice test with time constraints, with all guides, "open book."
5. Take a final practice test without open material and with time limits.

If you have time to take more practice tests, just repeat step 5. By gradually exposing yourself to the full rigors of the test environment, you will condition your mind to the stress of test day and maximize your success.

Secret Key #4 - Prepare, Don't Procrastinate

Let me state an obvious fact: if you take the test three times, you will probably get three different scores. This is due to the way you feel on test day, the level of preparedness you have, and the version of the test you see. Despite the test writers' claims to the contrary, some versions of the test WILL be easier for you than others.
Since your future depends so much on your score, you should maximize your chances of success. In order to maximize the likelihood of success, you've got to prepare in advance. This means taking practice tests and spending time learning the information and test taking strategies you will need to succeed.

Never go take the actual test as a "practice" test, expecting that you can just take it again if you need to. Take all the practice tests you can on your own, but when you go to take the official test, be prepared, be focused, and do your best the first time!

Secret Key #5 - Test Yourself

Everyone knows that time is money. There is no need to spend too much of your time or too little of your time preparing for the test. You should only spend as much of your precious time preparing as is necessary for you to get the score you need.

Once you have taken a practice test under real conditions of time constraints, then you will know if you are ready for the test or not.

If you have scored extremely high the first time that you take the practice test, then there is not much point in spending countless hours studying. You are already there.

Benchmark your abilities by retaking practice tests and seeing how much you have improved. Once you consistently score high enough to guarantee success, then you are ready.

If you have scored well below where you need, then knuckle down and begin studying in earnest. Check your improvement regularly through the use of practice tests under real conditions. Above all, don't worry, panic, or give up. The key is perseverance!

Then, when you go to take the test, remain confident and remember how well you did on the practice tests. If you can score high enough on a practice test, then you can do the same on the real thing.

General Strategies

The most important thing you can do is to ignore your fears and jump into the test immediately. Do not be overwhelmed by any strange-sounding terms. You have to jump into the test like jumping into a pool—all at once is the easiest way.

Make Predictions

As you read and understand the question, try to guess what the answer will be. Remember that several of the answer choices are wrong, and once you begin reading them, your mind will immediately become cluttered with answer choices designed to throw you off. Your mind is typically the most focused immediately after you have read the question and digested its contents. If you can, try to predict what the correct answer will be. You may be surprised at what you can predict.

Quickly scan the choices and see if your prediction is in the listed answer choices. If it is, then you can be quite confident that you have the right answer. It still won't hurt to check the other answer choices, but most of the time, you've got it!

Answer the Question

It may seem obvious to only pick answer choices that answer the question, but the test writers can create some excellent answer choices that are wrong. Don't pick an answer just because it sounds right, or you believe it to be true. It MUST answer the question. Once you've made your selection, always go back and check it against the question and make sure that you didn't misread the question and that the answer choice does answer the question posed.

Benchmark

After you read the first answer choice, decide if you think it sounds correct or not. If it doesn't, move on to the next answer choice. If it does, mentally mark that answer choice. This doesn't mean that you've definitely selected it as your answer choice, it just means that it's the best you've seen thus far. Go ahead and read the next choice. If the next choice is worse than the one you've already selected, keep going to the next answer choice. If the next choice is better than the choice you've already selected, mentally mark the new answer choice as your best guess.

The first answer choice that you select becomes your standard. Every other answer choice must be benchmarked against that standard. That choice is correct until proven otherwise by another answer choice beating it out. Once you've decided that no other answer choice seems as good, do one final check to ensure that your answer choice answers the question posed.

Valid Information

Don't discount any of the information provided in the question. Every piece of information may be necessary to determine the correct answer. None of the information in the question is there to throw you off (while the answer choices will certainly have information to throw you off). If two seemingly unrelated topics are discussed, don't ignore either. You can be confident there is a relationship, or it wouldn't be included in the question, and you are probably going to have to determine what is that relationship to find the answer.

Avoid "Fact Traps"

Don't get distracted by a choice that is factually true. Your search is for the answer that answers the question. Stay focused and don't fall for an answer that is true but irrelevant. Always go back to the question and make sure you're choosing an answer that actually answers the question and is not just a true statement. An answer can be factually correct, but it MUST answer the question asked. Additionally, two answers can both be seemingly correct, so be sure to read all of the answer choices, and make sure that you get the one that BEST answers the question.

Milk the Question

Some of the questions may throw you completely off. They might deal with a subject you have not been exposed to, or one that you haven't reviewed in years. While your lack of knowledge about the subject will be a hindrance, the question itself can give you many clues that will help you find the correct answer. Read the question carefully and look for clues. Watch particularly for adjectives and nouns describing difficult terms or words that you don't recognize. Regardless of whether you completely understand a word or not, replacing it with a synonym, either provided or one you more familiar with, may help you to understand what the questions are asking. Rather than wracking your mind about specific detailed information concerning a difficult term or word, try to use mental substitutes that are easier to understand.

The Trap of Familiarity

Don't just choose a word because you recognize it. On difficult questions, you may not recognize a number of words in the answer choices. The test writers don't put "make-believe" words on the test, so don't think that just because you only recognize all the words in one answer choice that that answer choice must be correct. If you only recognize words in one answer choice, then focus on that one. Is it correct? Try your best to determine if it is correct. If it is, that's great. If not, eliminate it. Each word and answer choice you eliminate increases your chances of getting the question correct, even if you then have to guess among the unfamiliar choices.

Eliminate Answers

Eliminate choices as soon as you realize they are wrong. But be careful! Make sure you consider all of the possible answer choices. Just because one appears right, doesn't mean that the next one won't be even better! The test writers will usually put more than one good answer choice for every question, so read all of them. Don't worry if you are stuck between two that seem right. By getting down to just two remaining possible choices, your odds are now 50/50. Rather than wasting too much time, play the odds. You are guessing, but guessing wisely because you've been able to knock out some of the answer choices that you know are wrong. If you are eliminating choices and realize that the last answer choice you are left with is also obviously wrong, don't panic. Start over and consider each choice again. There may easily be something that you missed the first time and will realize on the second pass.

Tough Questions

If you are stumped on a problem or it appears too hard or too difficult, don't waste time. Move on! Remember though, if you can quickly check for obviously incorrect answer choices, your chances of guessing correctly are greatly improved. Before you completely give up, at least try to knock out a couple of possible answers. Eliminate what you can and then guess at the remaining answer choices before moving on.

Brainstorm

If you get stuck on a difficult question, spend a few seconds quickly brainstorming. Run through the complete list of possible answer choices. Look at each choice and ask yourself, "Could this answer the question satisfactorily?" Go through each answer choice and consider it independently of the others. By systematically going through all possibilities, you may find something that you would otherwise overlook. Remember though that when you get stuck, it's important to try to keep moving.

Read Carefully

Understand the problem. Read the question and answer choices carefully. Don't miss the question because you misread the terms. You have plenty of time to read each question thoroughly and make sure you understand what is being asked. Yet a happy medium must be attained, so don't waste too much time. You must read carefully, but efficiently.

Face Value

When in doubt, use common sense. Always accept the situation in the problem at face value. Don't read too much into it. These problems will not require you to make huge leaps of logic. The test writers aren't trying to throw you off with a cheap trick. If you have to go beyond creativity and make a leap of logic in order to have an answer choice answer the question, then you should look at the other answer choices. Don't overcomplicate the problem by creating theoretical relationships or explanations that will warp time or space. These are normal problems rooted in reality. It's just that the applicable relationship or explanation may not be readily apparent and you have to figure things out. Use your common sense to interpret anything that isn't clear.

Prefixes

If you're having trouble with a word in the question or answer choices, try dissecting it. Take advantage of every clue that the word might include. Prefixes and suffixes can be a huge help. Usually they allow you to determine a basic meaning. Pre- means before, post- means after, pro - is positive, de- is negative. From these prefixes and suffixes, you can get an idea of the general meaning of the word and try to put it into context. Beware though of any traps. Just because con- is the opposite of pro-, doesn't necessarily mean congress is the opposite of progress!

Hedge Phrases

Watch out for critical hedge phrases, led off with words such as "likely," "may," "can," "sometimes," "often," "almost," "mostly," "usually," "generally," "rarely," and "sometimes." Question writers insert these hedge phrases to cover every possibility. Often an answer choice will be wrong simply because it leaves no room for exception. Unless the situation calls for them, avoid answer choices that have definitive words like "exactly," and "always."

Switchback Words

Stay alert for "switchbacks." These are the words and phrases frequently used to alert you to shifts in thought. The most common switchback word is "but." Others include "although," "however," "nevertheless," "on the other hand," "even though," "while," "in spite of," "despite," and "regardless of."

New Information

Correct answer choices will rarely have completely new information included. Answer choices typically are straightforward reflections of the material asked about and will directly relate to the question. If a new piece of information is included in an answer choice that doesn't even seem to relate to the topic being asked about, then that answer choice is likely incorrect. All of the information needed to answer the question is usually provided for you in the question. You should not have to make guesses that are unsupported or choose answer choices that require unknown information that cannot be reasoned from what is given.

Time Management

On technical questions, don't get lost on the technical terms. Don't spend too much time on any one question. If you don't know what a term means, then odds are you aren't going to get much further since you don't have a dictionary. You should be able to immediately recognize whether or not you know a term. If you don't, work with the other clues that you have—the other answer choices and terms provided—but don't waste too much time trying to figure out a difficult term that you don't know.

Contextual Clues

Look for contextual clues. An answer can be right but not the correct answer. The contextual clues will help you find the answer that is most right and is correct. Understand the context in which a phrase or statement is made. This will help you make important distinctions.

Don't Panic

Panicking will not answer any questions for you; therefore, it isn't helpful. When you first see the question, if your mind goes blank, take a deep breath. Force yourself to mechanically go through the steps of solving the problem using the strategies you've learned.

Pace Yourself

Don't get clock fever. It's easy to be overwhelmed when you're looking at a page full of questions, your mind is full of random thoughts and feeling confused, and the clock is ticking down faster than you would like. Calm down and maintain the pace that you have set for yourself. As long as you are on track by monitoring your pace, you are guaranteed to have enough time for yourself. When you get to the last few minutes of the test, it may seem like you won't have enough time left, but if you only have as many questions as you should have left at that point, then you're right on track!

Answer Selection

The best way to pick an answer choice is to eliminate all of those that are wrong, until only one is left and confirm that is the correct answer. Sometimes though, an answer choice may immediately look right. Be careful! Take a second to make sure that the other choices are not equally obvious. Don't make a hasty mistake. There are only two times that you should stop before checking other answers. First is when you are positive that the answer choice you have selected is correct. Second is when time is almost out and you have to make a quick guess!

Check Your Work

Since you will probably not know every term listed and the answer to every question, it is important that you get credit for the ones that you do know. Don't miss any questions through careless mistakes. If at all possible, try to take a second to look back over your answer selection and make sure you've selected the correct answer choice and haven't made a costly careless mistake (such as marking an answer choice that you didn't mean to mark). The time it takes for this quick double check should more than pay for itself in caught mistakes.

Beware of Directly Quoted Answers

Sometimes an answer choice will repeat word for word a portion of the question or reference section. However, beware of such exact duplication. It may be a trap! More than likely, the correct choice will paraphrase or summarize a point, rather than being exactly the same wording.

Slang

Scientific sounding answers are better than slang ones. An answer choice that begins "To compare the outcomes..." is much more likely to be correct than one that begins "Because some people insisted..."

Extreme Statements

Avoid wild answers that throw out highly controversial ideas that are proclaimed as established fact. An answer choice that states the "process should used in certain situations, if..." is much more likely to be correct than one that states the "process should be discontinued completely." The first is a calm rational statement and doesn't even make a definitive, uncompromising stance, using a hedge word "if" to provide wiggle room, whereas the second choice is a radical idea and far more extreme.

Answer Choice Families

When you have two or more answer choices that are direct opposites or parallels, one of them is usually the correct answer. For instance, if one answer choice states "x increases" and another answer choice states "x decreases" or "y increases," then those two or three answer choices are very similar in construction and fall into the same family of answer choices. A family of answer choices consists of two or three answer choices, very similar in construction, but often with directly opposite meanings. Usually the correct answer choice will be in that family of answer choices. The "odd man out" or answer choice that doesn't seem to fit the parallel construction of the other answer choices is more likely to be incorrect.

Special Report: How to Overcome Test Anxiety

The very nature of tests caters to some level of anxiety, nervousness, or tension, just as we feel for any important event that occurs in our lives. A little bit of anxiety or nervousness can be a good thing. It helps us with motivation, and makes achievement just that much sweeter. However, too much anxiety can be a problem, especially if it hinders our ability to function and perform.

"Test anxiety," is the term that refers to the emotional reactions that some test-takers experience when faced with a test or exam. Having a fear of testing and exams is based upon a rational fear, since the test-taker's performance can shape the course of an academic career. Nevertheless, experiencing excessive fear of examinations will only interfere with the test-taker's ability to perform and chance to be successful.

There are a large variety of causes that can contribute to the development and sensation of test anxiety. These include, but are not limited to, lack of preparation and worrying about issues surrounding the test.

Lack of Preparation

Lack of preparation can be identified by the following behaviors or situations:

Not scheduling enough time to study, and therefore cramming the night before the test or exam
Managing time poorly, to create the sensation that there is not enough time to do everything
Failing to organize the text information in advance, so that the study material consists of the entire text and not simply the pertinent information
Poor overall studying habits

Worrying, on the other hand, can be related to both the test taker, or many other factors around him/her that will be affected by the results of the test. These include worrying about:

Previous performances on similar exams, or exams in general
How friends and other students are achieving
The negative consequences that will result from a poor grade or failure

There are three primary elements to test anxiety. Physical components, which involve the same typical bodily reactions as those to acute anxiety (to be discussed below). Emotional factors have to do with fear or panic. Mental or cognitive issues concerning attention spans and memory abilities.

Physical Signals

There are many different symptoms of test anxiety, and these are not limited to mental and emotional strain. Frequently there are a range of physical signals that will let a test taker know that he/she is suffering from test anxiety. These bodily changes can include the following:

Perspiring
Sweaty palms
Wet, trembling hands
Nausea
Dry mouth
A knot in the stomach
Headache
Faintness
Muscle tension
Aching shoulders, back and neck
Rapid heart beat
Feeling too hot/cold

To recognize the sensation of test anxiety, a test-taker should monitor him/herself for the following sensations:

The physical distress symptoms as listed above
Emotional sensitivity, expressing emotional feelings such as the need to cry or laugh too much, or a sensation of anger or helplessness
A decreased ability to think, causing the test-taker to blank out or have racing thoughts that are hard to organize or control.

Though most students will feel some level of anxiety when faced with a test or exam, the majority can cope with that anxiety and maintain it at a manageable level. However, those who cannot are faced with a very real and very serious condition, which can and should be controlled for the immeasurable benefit of this sufferer.

Naturally, these sensations lead to negative results for the testing experience. The most common effects of test anxiety have to do with nervousness and mental blocking.

Nervousness

Nervousness can appear in several different levels:

The test-taker's difficulty, or even inability to read and understand the questions on the test
The difficulty or inability to organize thoughts to a coherent form
The difficulty or inability to recall key words and concepts relating to the testing questions (especially essays)
The receipt of poor grades on a test, though the test material was well known by the test taker

Conversely, a person may also experience mental blocking, which involves:

Blanking out on test questions
Only remembering the correct answers to the questions when the test has already finished.

Fortunately for test anxiety sufferers, beating these feelings, to a large degree, has to do with proper preparation. When a test taker has a feeling of preparedness, then anxiety will be dramatically lessened.

The first step to resolving anxiety issues is to distinguish which of the two types of anxiety are being suffered. If the anxiety is a direct result of a lack of preparation, this should be considered a normal reaction, and the anxiety level (as opposed to the test results) shouldn't be anything to worry about. However, if, when adequately prepared, the test-taker still panics, blanks out, or seems to overreact, this is not a fully rational reaction. While this can be considered normal too, there are many ways to combat and overcome these effects.

Remember that anxiety cannot be entirely eliminated, however, there are ways to minimize it, to make the anxiety easier to manage. Preparation is one of the best ways to minimize test anxiety. Therefore the following techniques are wise in order to best fight off any anxiety that may want to build.

To begin with, try to avoid cramming before a test, whenever it is possible. By trying to memorize an entire term's worth of information in one day, you'll be shocking your system, and not giving yourself a very good chance to absorb the information. This is an easy path to anxiety, so for those who suffer from test anxiety, cramming should not even be considered an option.

Instead of cramming, work throughout the semester to combine all of the material which is presented throughout the semester, and work on it gradually as the course goes by, making sure to master the main concepts first, leaving minor details for a week or so before the test.

To study for the upcoming exam, be sure to pose questions that may be on the examination, to gauge the ability to answer them by integrating the ideas from your texts, notes and lectures, as well as any supplementary readings.

If it is truly impossible to cover all of the information that was covered in that particular term, concentrate on the most important portions, that can be covered very well. Learn these concepts as best as possible, so that when the test comes, a goal can be made to use these concepts as presentations of your knowledge.

In addition to study habits, changes in attitude are critical to beating a struggle with test anxiety. In fact, an improvement of the perspective over the entire test-taking experience can actually help a test taker to enjoy studying and therefore improve the overall experience. Be certain not to overemphasize the significance of the grade - know that the result of the test is neither a reflection of self worth, nor is it a measure of intelligence; one grade will not predict a person's future success.

- 125 -

To improve an overall testing outlook, the following steps should be tried:

Keeping in mind that the most reasonable expectation for taking a test is to expect to try to demonstrate as much of what you know as you possibly can.
Reminding ourselves that a test is only one test; this is not the only one, and there will be others.
The thought of thinking of oneself in an irrational, all-or-nothing term should be avoided at all costs.
A reward should be designated for after the test, so there's something to look forward to. Whether it be going to a movie, going out to eat, or simply visiting friends, schedule it in advance, and do it no matter what result is expected on the exam.

Test-takers should also keep in mind that the basics are some of the most important things, even beyond anti-anxiety techniques and studying. Never neglect the basic social, emotional and biological needs, in order to try to absorb information. In order to best achieve, these three factors must be held as just as important as the studying itself.

Study Steps

Remember the following important steps for studying:

Maintain healthy nutrition and exercise habits. Continue both your recreational activities and social pass times. These both contribute to your physical and emotional well being.
Be certain to get a good amount of sleep, especially the night before the test, because when you're overtired you are not able to perform to the best of your best ability.
Keep the studying pace to a moderate level by taking breaks when they are needed, and varying the work whenever possible, to keep the mind fresh instead of getting bored.
When enough studying has been done that all the material that can be learned has been learned, and the test taker is prepared for the test, stop studying and do something relaxing such as listening to music, watching a movie, or taking a warm bubble bath.

There are also many other techniques to minimize the uneasiness or apprehension that is experienced along with test anxiety before, during, or even after the examination. In fact, there are a great deal of things that can be done to stop anxiety from interfering with lifestyle and performance. Again, remember that anxiety will not be eliminated entirely, and it shouldn't be. Otherwise that "up" feeling for exams would not exist, and most of us depend on that sensation to perform better than usual. However, this anxiety has to be at a level that is manageable.

Of course, as we have just discussed, being prepared for the exam is half the battle right away. Attending all classes, finding out what knowledge will be expected on the exam, and knowing the exam schedules are easy steps to lowering anxiety. Keeping up with work will remove the need to cram, and efficient study habits will eliminate wasted time. Studying should be done in an ideal location for concentration, so that it is simple to become interested in the material and give it complete attention. A method such as SQ3R (Survey, Question, Read, Recite, Review) is a wonderful key to follow to make sure that the study habits are as effective as possible, especially in the case of learning from a textbook. Flashcards are great techniques for memorization. Learning to take good notes will mean that notes will be full of useful information, so that less sifting will need to be done to seek out what is pertinent for studying. Reviewing notes after class and then again on occasion will keep the information fresh in the mind. From notes that have been taken summary sheets and outlines can be made for simpler reviewing.

A study group can also be a very motivational and helpful place to study, as there will be a sharing of ideas, all of the minds can work together, to make sure that everyone understands, and the studying will be made more interesting because it will be a social occasion.

Basically, though, as long as the test-taker remains organized and self confident, with efficient study habits, less time will need to be spent studying, and higher grades will be achieved.

To become self confident, there are many useful steps. The first of these is "self talk." It has been shown through extensive research, that self-talk for students who suffer from test anxiety, should be well monitored, in order to make sure that it contributes to self confidence as opposed to sinking the student. Frequently the self talk of test-anxious students is negative or self-defeating, thinking that everyone else is smarter and faster, that they always mess up, and that if they don't do well, they'll fail the entire course. It is important to decreasing anxiety that awareness is made of self talk. Try writing any negative self thoughts and then disputing them with a positive statement instead. Begin self-encouragement as though it was a friend speaking. Repeat positive statements to help reprogram the mind to believing in successes instead of failures.

Helpful Techniques

Other extremely helpful techniques include:

Self-visualization of doing well and reaching goals
While aiming for an "A" level of understanding, don't try to "overprotect" by setting your expectations lower. This will only convince the mind to stop studying in order to meet the lower expectations.
Don't make comparisons with the results or habits of other students. These are individual factors, and different things work for different people, causing different results.
Strive to become an expert in learning what works well, and what can be done in order to improve. Consider collecting this data in a journal.
Create rewards for after studying instead of doing things before studying that will only turn into avoidance behaviors.
Make a practice of relaxing - by using methods such as progressive relaxation, self-hypnosis, guided imagery, etc - in order to make relaxation an automatic sensation.
Work on creating a state of relaxed concentration so that concentrating will take on the focus of the mind, so that none will be wasted on worrying.
Take good care of the physical self by eating well and getting enough sleep.
Plan in time for exercise and stick to this plan.

Beyond these techniques, there are other methods to be used before, during and after the test that will help the test-taker perform well in addition to overcoming anxiety.

Before the exam comes the academic preparation. This involves establishing a study schedule and beginning at least one week before the actual date of the test. By doing this, the anxiety of not having enough time to study for the test will be automatically eliminated. Moreover, this will make the studying a much more effective experience, ensuring that the learning will be an easier process. This relieves much undue pressure on the test-taker.

Summary sheets, note cards, and flash cards with the main concepts and examples of these main concepts should be prepared in advance of the actual studying time. A topic should never be eliminated from this process. By omitting a topic because it isn't expected to be on the test is only setting up the test-taker for anxiety should it actually appear on the exam. Utilize the course syllabus for laying out the topics that should be studied. Carefully go over the notes that were made in class, paying special attention to any of the issues that the professor took special care to emphasize while lecturing in class. In the textbooks, use the chapter review, or if possible, the chapter tests, to begin your review.

It may even be possible to ask the instructor what information will be covered on the exam, or what the format of the exam will be (for example, multiple choice, essay, free form, true-false). Additionally, see if it is possible to find out how many questions will be on the test. If a review sheet or sample test has been offered by the professor, make good use of it, above anything else, for the preparation for the test. Another great resource for getting to know the examination is reviewing tests from previous semesters. Use these tests to review, and aim to achieve a 100% score on each of the possible topics. With a few exceptions, the goal that you set for yourself is the highest one that you will reach.

Take all of the questions that were assigned as homework, and rework them to any other possible course material. The more problems reworked, the more skill and confidence will form as a result. When forming the solution to a problem, write out each of the steps. Don't simply do head work. By doing as many steps on paper as possible, much clarification and therefore confidence will be formed. Do this with as many homework problems as possible, before checking the answers. By checking the answer after each problem, a reinforcement will exist, that will not be on the exam. Study situations should be as exam-like as possible, to prime the test-taker's system for the experience. By waiting to check the answers at the end, a psychological advantage will be formed, to decrease the stress factor.

Another fantastic reason for not cramming is the avoidance of confusion in concepts, especially when it comes to mathematics. 8-10 hours of study will become one hundred percent more effective if it is spread out over a week or at least several days, instead of doing it all in one sitting. Recognize that the human brain requires time in order to assimilate new material, so frequent breaks and a span of study time over several days will be much more beneficial.

Additionally, don't study right up until the point of the exam. Studying should stop a minimum of one hour before the exam begins. This allows the brain to rest and put things in their proper order. This will also provide the time to become as relaxed as possible when going into the examination room. The test-taker will also have time to eat well and eat sensibly. Know that the brain needs food as much as the rest of the body. With enough food and enough sleep, as well as a relaxed attitude, the body and the mind are primed for success.

Avoid any anxious classmates who are talking about the exam. These students only spread anxiety, and are not worth sharing the anxious sentimentalities.

Before the test also involves creating a positive attitude, so mental preparation should also be a point of concentration. There are many keys to creating a positive attitude. Should fears become rushing in, make a visualization of taking the exam, doing well, and seeing an A written on the paper. Write out a list of affirmations that will bring a feeling of confidence, such as "I am doing well in my English class," "I studied well and know my material," "I enjoy this class." Even if the affirmations aren't believed at first, it sends a positive message to the subconscious which will result in an alteration of the overall belief system, which is the system that creates reality.

If a sensation of panic begins, work with the fear and imagine the very worst! Work through the entire scenario of not passing the test, failing the entire course, and dropping out of school, followed by not getting a job, and pushing a shopping cart through the dark alley where you'll live. This will place things into perspective! Then, practice deep breathing and create a visualization of the opposite situation - achieving an "A" on the exam, passing the entire course, receiving the degree at a graduation ceremony.

On the day of the test, there are many things to be done to ensure the best results, as well as the most calm outlook. The following stages are suggested in order to maximize test-taking potential:

Begin the examination day with a moderate breakfast, and avoid any coffee or beverages with caffeine if the test taker is prone to jitters. Even people who are used to managing caffeine can feel jittery or light-headed when it is taken on a test day.
Attempt to do something that is relaxing before the examination begins. As last minute cramming clouds the mastering of overall concepts, it is better to use this time to create a calming outlook.
Be certain to arrive at the test location well in advance, in order to provide time to select a location that is away from doors, windows and other distractions, as well as giving enough time to relax before the test begins.
Keep away from anxiety generating classmates who will upset the sensation of stability and relaxation that is being attempted before the exam.
Should the waiting period before the exam begins cause anxiety, create a self-distraction by reading a light magazine or something else that is relaxing and simple.

During the exam itself, read the entire exam from beginning to end, and find out how much time should be allotted to each individual problem. Once writing the exam, should more time be taken for a problem, it should be abandoned, in order to begin another problem. If there is time at the end, the unfinished problem can always be returned to and completed.

Read the instructions very carefully - twice - so that unpleasant surprises won't follow during or after the exam has ended.

When writing the exam, pretend that the situation is actually simply the completion of homework within a library, or at home. This will assist in forming a relaxed atmosphere, and will allow the brain extra focus for the complex thinking function.

Begin the exam with all of the questions with which the most confidence is felt. This will build the confidence level regarding the entire exam and will begin a quality momentum. This will also create encouragement for trying the problems where uncertainty resides.

Going with the "gut instinct" is always the way to go when solving a problem. Second guessing should be avoided at all costs. Have confidence in the ability to do well.

For essay questions, create an outline in advance that will keep the mind organized and make certain that all of the points are remembered. For multiple choice, read every answer, even if the correct one has been spotted - a better one may exist.

Continue at a pace that is reasonable and not rushed, in order to be able to work carefully. Provide enough time to go over the answers at the end, to check for small errors that can be corrected.

Should a feeling of panic begin, breathe deeply, and think of the feeling of the body releasing sand through its pores. Visualize a calm, peaceful place, and include all of the sights, sounds and sensations of this image. Continue the deep breathing, and take a few minutes to continue this with closed eyes. When all is well again, return to the test.

If a "blanking" occurs for a certain question, skip it and move on to the next question. There will be time to return to the other question later. Get everything done that can be done, first, to guarantee all the grades that can be compiled, and to build all of the confidence possible. Then return to the weaker questions to build the marks from there.

Remember, one's own reality can be created, so as long as the belief is there, success will follow. And remember: anxiety can happen later, right now, there's an exam to be written!

After the examination is complete, whether there is a feeling for a good grade or a bad grade, don't dwell on the exam, and be certain to follow through on the reward that was promised...and enjoy it! Don't dwell on any mistakes that have been made, as there is nothing that can be done at this point anyway.

Additionally, don't begin to study for the next test right away. Do something relaxing for a while, and let the mind relax and prepare itself to begin absorbing information again.

From the results of the exam - both the grade and the entire experience, be certain to learn from what has gone on. Perfect studying habits and work some more on confidence in order to make the next examination experience even better than the last one.

Learn to avoid places where openings occurred for laziness, procrastination and day dreaming.

Use the time between this exam and the next one to better learn to relax, even learning to relax on cue, so that any anxiety can be controlled during the next exam. Learn how to relax the body. Slouch in your chair if that helps. Tighten and then relax all of the different muscle groups, one group at a time, beginning with the feet and then working all the way up to the neck and face. This will ultimately relax the muscles more than they were to begin with. Learn how to breathe deeply and comfortably, and focus on this breathing going in and out as a relaxing thought. With every exhale, repeat the word "relax."

As common as test anxiety is, it is very possible to overcome it. Make yourself one of the test-takers who overcome this frustrating hindrance.

Special Report: Additional Bonus Material

Due to our efforts to try to keep this book to a manageable length, we've created a link that will give you access to all of your additional bonus material.

Please visit http://www.mometrix.com/bonus948/clephumgrodev to access the information.